WHERE SIN ABOUNDS

WHERE SIN ABOUNDS

A Religious History of Las Vegas

STANLEY A. STEWARD

WIPF & STOCK · Eugene, Oregon

WHERE SIN ABOUNDS
A Religious History of Las Vegas

Wipf & Stock
An Imprint of Wipf and Stock Publishers
199 W. 8th Ave., Suite 3
Eugene, OR 97401

www.wipfandstock.com

ISBN 13: 978-1-61097-017-4

Cataloging-in-Publication data:

Steward, Stanley A.

Where sin abounds : a religious history of Las Vegas / Stanley A. Steward.

viii + 158 p. ; 23 cm. Includes bibliographical references.

ISBN 13: 978-1-61097-017-4

1. Las Vegas (Nev.)—History—20th century. 2. Pentecostalism—History. 3. Christianity—United States. I. Title.

BR1644 S302 2012

Manufactured in the U.S.A.

1

The Pentecostal Tradition

WHEN THINKING OF LAS Vegas, images of gambling, casinos, showgirls, world-class entertainers, and dazzling lights come to mind. Few people associate religion with "Sin City." However, Las Vegas includes a vibrant religious community that has always existed on the shadow side of the neon. Nationally, Pentecostalism has been the fastest growing religion of the twentieth century. Several surveys concluded the number of Pentecostals grew from zero to hundreds of millions in just ninety years, and by 1990 the Pentecostals had become one of the most prominent religious groups in Las Vegas. This study will concentrate on the dynamic relationship between Las Vegas Pentecostals and the city's entertainment industry.

A broad definition of Pentecostals, charismatics, and evangelicals will be helpful in understanding the effects of Pentecostalism in Las Vegas. On many points of doctrine, evangelicals and charismatics believe the same thing. They accept the full deity of Jesus Christ, his virgin birth, his atoning work, and Jesus' bodily resurrection. The Bible is considered to be the inerrant, infallible, inspired word of God and is absolutely authoritative.[1] Charismatics and evangelicals both adhere to the reality of heaven and hell and maintain that salvation comes through Christ alone. According to their theology, the world's only real hope lies in the promised return of Christ.[2] Theirs is a fundamentally dualistic world view with the present age existing in a tension between the forces of good and evil.

Another common characteristic includes an insistence upon a personal born-again experience. To be born again means to make a personal,

1. Pearlman, *Knowing the Doctrines of the Bible*, 19–21.
2. Weber, *Living in the Shadow of the Second Coming*, 82–104.

1

conscious decision to renounce one's old way of life and accept Jesus Christ as Lord. It is usually called "getting saved." In addition, charismatics, and evangelicals share an emphasis on personal piety. The validity of one's Christianity is measured by lifestyle and behavioral choices.

There is an intangible but very powerful appeal to the personal and shared experience of many evangelicals and charismatics. It involves a passion for their religion and an enthusiasm that translates into a worldview and a powerful evangelistic zeal. Their faith is a profound personal reality and not simply a relative or contextual set of abstract beliefs. Their personal passion has generated an activist brand of Christianity.

The only point distinguishing the two conservative Christian movements is the theology of the Holy Spirit. Charismatics emphasize the present-day operation of the Spirit in the life of the believer. Spirit baptism, as evidenced by speaking "in other tongues," and the manifestation of spiritual gifts such as healing, miracles, and prophecy are also regarded as legitimate present-day activities of the Spirit. In contrast, a lot of evangelicals do not believe such works of the Spirit are for today. Many evangelicals do not regard themselves as charismatic, but charismatics consider themselves part of the broader evangelical community. It is important to note several Pentecostal denominations are members of the National Association of Evangelicals.

Just as evangelicals and charismatics are not synonymous, neither are charismatics identical with classical Pentecostals. Classical Pentecostals are those who have roots in the birth of the modern Pentecostal movement that occurred early in the twentieth century. Pentecostals formed denominations of their own. They tend to take a dogmatic stand concerning "tongues" as the universal initial physical evidence of Spirit baptism. Charismatics, on the other hand, often times retain affiliation in denominational churches and tend to take a less absolute view concerning Spirit baptism. Charismatics fully believe in the present-day work of the Holy Spirit but regard tongues as just one evidence of Spirit baptism. Charismatics and Pentecostals generally enjoy a friendly sibling relationship; therefore, the terms "Pentecostal" and "charismatic" will be used interchangeably.

This study will concentrate mostly on Pentecostalism in the Las Vegas Valley between 1928 and 1990. The only time the scope will be broadened is in chapter 6, which examines the revival on the Las Vegas Strip. The events of that period flowed over the banks of classical Pentecostalism and infiltrated evangelicals and charismatics. The chapter will survey the broad religious heritage of Las Vegas in general and then the presence of Pentecostals in particular in this desert oasis. It will not attempt to cover all Pentecostal churches or denominations but will focus on some of the most prominent expressions of the movement on the local scene. There will also be an analysis of diverse personalities and groups within the city in an effort to represent local Pentecostals as a whole.

To this end, an effort will be made to explain the response of various ethnic groups including Anglos, African Americans, Koreans, and Latinos. It should be noted that while Hispanics constituted the fastest-growing segment of the local population after 1990, they were only a fractional minority up until that time. A post-1990 study would need to emphasize them more. Women have historically been at the forefront of the Pentecostalism, and they will constitute a prominent dimension in this study. Special attention will be devoted to the relationship between Pentecostalism and aspects of Las Vegas' entertainment industry.

This book represents part of the recent trend in American religious historiography to situate evangelicals and charismatics in the development of modern Christianity in the United States. Nathan Hatch, for instance, explored the connection between evangelicalism and the American democratic ethos. His thesis is that the religious movement out of which Pentecostalism emerged has contributed in a major way to the growth of American democracy. Harold Bloom, in *The American Religion*, and Paul Conklin, in *American Originals*, has shown that Americans originated a number of configurations of faith. Among the American originals were Pentecostals.

Paul Johnson, in *Shopkeeper's Millennium*, maintained that the old Marxist control theory of religion does not adequately explain this democratic-type American religion. His case study focused on the early nineteenth-century revival in Rochester, New York. He demonstrated that religion in this formative period of American culture was, at least in part, a people's movement. It was motivated more by the desire for self-control rather than an attempt by the social elite to fashion the behavior of the lower economic class. The Holy Spirit religionists of the twentieth century were also democratically motivated and organized. Their churches were sovereign corporations regulated by a congregational form of church government. Their pastors were elected by parishioners and funding almost always depended upon the freewill offerings of congregants. There were no parent organizations or ecclesiastical hierarchies that provided money. They were owned and operated at the local level.

Robert Mapes Anderson, in *Vision of the Disinherited*, contended Pentecostals represent a case study in upward mobility. He traced their roots to the disenfranchised citizens of American society. An outsider status shaped their theology, their hope, and their view of American culture as a whole.[3] However, as their standing in society changed for the better, their understanding of the relationship between Christ and culture evolved.

Grant Wacker identified pragmatism as a distinguishing characteristic of the Pentecostal psyche. His recent book *Heaven Below* made this point. He maintained that, at the end of the day, Pentecostals proved remarkably willing to work within the social and cultural expectations of the age. They held a proverbial finger to the wind, calculated where they were, where they wanted to go and, above all, how to get there. Their ability to figure the odds and react appropriately made them pragmatists to the bone.[4]

In his book *The Restructuring of Religion* in America Robert Wuthnow claimed Evangelical/Pentecostal faith was fast becoming the new religion of the American mainstream. As traditional Protestant denominations slipped into decline, the new Evangelical/Pentecostal formations of faith were on the ascent. It was not only in America that Pentecostalism was on the rise. It truly had an international flavor and spread to every inhabited continent on the globe. However, although its constituency cut across ethnic barriers, indigenous groups tended to cluster along ethnic lines. Las Vegas Pentecostals followed the Azusa Street pattern in that they, at first, worshipped as an interracial-group but gradually drifted into separate, more ethnically exclusive, churches.

Pentecostalism is an experientially-based spirituality. It is a personal encounter with the Divine that defines a distinctive brand of religion. It is not bound by formalism, liturgy, or tradition. Harvey Cox described Pentecostals as a "spiritual hurricane" that has already touched a half billion people. Pentecostals offer an alternative vision of the human future whose impact may only be in its earliest stages. For Pentecostals, genuine

---

3. Anderson, *Vision of the Disinherited*, 228–29.

4. Wacker, *Heaven Below*, 13–14.

religion is a dynamic relationship with a living God through the medium of the Holy Spirit.[5]

Mine Eyes Have Seen the Glory, by Randal Balmer, pioneered a new method of studying religion in America. Rather than relying on church records and written documentation alone, he visited various Evangelical/ Pentecostal churches and communities in formulating the text of his study of this sub-culture in modern America. His up-close and personal approach provided valuable insight into the question of why these groups have had such an impact. Balmer's methodology will be utilized in this study of Pentecostalism in the Las Vegas Valley. Written documentation and church records were employed when available, but there was much information gathered through personal interviews and oral history. This style of research was employed for two reasons. First, written data was not always available, since many churches did not keep careful records of their past. There was some written history available concerning the oldest churches in Las Vegas and that documentation was utilized. Second, oral history made more realistic the churches and individuals under consideration. Pentecostalism is an existentialist spirituality. First-hand accounts capture its essence better than mere statistical analysis.

This study will seek to validate the claim that religion has been an integral part of the town-making process in Las Vegas. It will trace the numerical growth and diversity within the local Pentecostal community and will demonstrate the pragmatic dimension of Pentecostalism that has enabled the movement to effectively adapt to new audiences. This book will contend that Las Vegas Pentecostalism has been an upwardly mobile movement. Many of its members have moved from the economic and social margins of the local community to the mainstream. Of particular interest will be the paradoxical relationship between piestic-minded Pentecostals and the Strip. Many spirit-filled believers found a way to integrate the two. How? As the story unfolds, it will show that sometimes Pentecostals were characterized by such noble themes as local community involvement, the struggle for social justice, and genuine concern for hurting people. However, in other instances they were given to moral compromise, egomania, greed, and power. All this figured into the mix of a rapidly growing movement that continues to assimilate into the American mainstream.

5. Cox, *Fire From Heaven*, 6.

2

Las Vegas Old Time Religion

CHRISTIANITY IS NO STRANGER to the Silver State. The faith arrived in Nevada long before any European settlement. Spanish Catholic missionaries and fur trappers were the first white arrivals in the West. The first Catholic mass was offered along the banks of the Colorado River south of present-day Laughlin by noted trailblazer Father Francisco Garces in 1775.[1] The Euro-Americans were not the only ones who engaged in religious activity in the Southwest. Native American Shoshone and Paiutes practiced their religions for hundreds of years before the Europeans arrived. When the Mormons came to the Las Vegas Valley in 1855 to establish a way station for travelers plying the trail between southern Utah and the newly-purchased (1851) Mormon ranch at San Bernardino, they established a mission to convert local Paiutes to Christianity. Even when Senator William Clark established his railroad town a half century later, religion continued to influence the valley's population.

When Clark's town site opened, it became an instant tent city populated by almost two thousand people. Early records indicate there were fourteen saloons among the businesses.[2] Senator Clark wrote to Dr. John Wesley Bain suggesting Dr. Bain, a university graduate and an ordained Southern Methodist Episcopal minister, come to Las Vegas to organize a congregation and build a church.[3] A side-boarded tent school served as the first home for the fledgling congregation. Sunday school was held at 10:00 a.m. and a preaching service at 11:00 a.m. The church formed with sixteen charter members. There were other Christians in Las Vegas, so the

---

1. *Diocean Directory*, 11.
2. Marshall, *First United Methodist Las Vegas*, 14.
3. *The Nevadan*. No author cited. This is Great Country, April 15, 1968, 4.

Methodist church served as a host congregation for all of them. Catholics, Mormons, Baptists, and Episcopalians all shared the facility and often worshiped together until each denomination launched its own church.[4]

Between 1920 and 1940, the local population increased from 2,304 to 8,600.[5] Churches quickly established themselves as a vital component of the growing community. It was especially important in the lives of parents who wanted their children to associate with a church. A local school census in 1906 reported 218 children eligible for school, with Sunday school attendance the same year showing an enrollment of 140 children.[6]

First Methodist church of Las Vegas had a mission mentality from the beginning. Reverend J. W. Bain, besides pastoring his local congregation, began conducting weekday services in Caliente and Logan in the Moapa valley. While this was taking place, a permanent church structure was planned and built in 1908.[7] The congregation continued as a vital part of Las Vegas as the community matured. Disaster struck in 1922 when a fire gutted the church building, but townspeople came to the rescue and organized a community-wide fundraising campaign that netted $10 thousand in pledges.[8]

First Methodist continued to enjoy a supportive and symbiotic relationship with the community. It maintained a close friendship with the Eagles Lodge, established the local Y.M.C.A., organized a Boy Scout Troop, and launched the mission that created Zion Methodist Church. In those days, it was not generally accepted for blacks and whites to worship together, so the launching of Zion might have been as much a testament to the racism of the day as a statement of the church's broad mission consciousness. In later years, other local Methodist congregations eclipsed the prominence of First Methodist. As the town expanded physically, the church more and more became a smaller downtown church with larger Methodist congregations emerging in the growing neighborhoods.

The second church to officially organize was Christ Episcopal, which formed in 1907. Until that time, the town's smattering of Episcopalians

4. Marshall, *First United Methodist Las Vegas*, 16.

5. U.S. Department of Commerce, Bureau of the Census, *Census of Population, 1920–1960*.

6. Marshall, First United Methodist Las Vegas, 14–19.

7. Ibid., 19.

8. Ibid., 36–38.

met with the Methodists. Nevada's Episcopalians were part of the Salt Lake diocese. After meeting with local Episcopalians, Bishop Franklin Spaulding selected Reverend Harry Gray, a recent graduate of Harvard Divinity School, as the first rector of the Las Vegas congregation.[9] The congregation quickly organized, and the Las Vegas Land and Water Company donated the railroad's substation for a church building. Local Episcopalians were a small but influential congregation. They emphasized community involvement as a dimension of genuine Christian witness. Their ranks consisted of business and community leaders including the publishers of the *Las Vegas Age*.[10] Although the church facility was small, it was well appointed. For instance, the Meneely Bell Company, recognized as the finest in the world, manufactured bells for the church.[11]

Christ Episcopal struggled during the early years. For a time, it was uncertain whether or not it would survive. Although it was never a particularly large congregation, it actively supported the creation of other southern Nevada missions. Christ Episcopal organized a Sunday school at Goodsprings and established the Epiphany Mission in Moapa. Church records indicate women played an active role. Indeed, there were numerous women's groups, and they were usually active in various fund raising activities. From 1952 to 1955, Christ Episcopal Church also became embroiled in the growing controversy over whether or not ministers should participate in the emerging wedding industry in Las Vegas. Reverend Malcolm Jones was expelled from the Clark County Ministerial Association because he refused to support the majority view requiring a minister be affiliated with a recognized church in order to perform weddings.[12] Throughout its history, Christ's Church blended with the mainstream culture and functioned as a friend of the community.

Catholicism was also an influential religion in the city. Southern Nevada had no Catholic parish when Father Lawrence Scanlon visited in 1905. Occasionally, visiting priests held mass outdoors or in a rented building. In 1906, Father Reynolds came to live in Las Vegas, but his territory included all of Southern Nevada. His immediate concern for Las

---

9. Squires, *Christ Church Episcopal*, 4.

10. Jones, Christ Church Episcopal 1907–1982, 3.

11. Ibid.

12. Ibid., 12–13.

Vegas was to secure funding to build a permanent church. Construction of St. Joan of Arc finally began in 1908.

Everything had to be done in the parishioners' spare time, but they were determined to have the church finished by Christmas. Towards the end of 1908 even the women were helping to hammer nails and carry wood. Reynolds held the first mass in the new church on Christmas Day 1908.[13] St. Joan of Arc served not only as a church but also has a community center. The congregation grew with the population of Las Vegas and, by 1940, had outgrown its original building. The Catholics built the present St. Joan of Arc facility directly in front of the old church and moved the latter to North Las Vegas where it served as the temporary home for the new St. Christopher parish.[14] Las Vegas Catholics, under the ecclesiastical jurisdiction of the Diocese of Salt Lake City, enjoyed a small but growing presence in the valley during the 1930s. As more Catholics arrived, there was the need for another church. Construction began on St. James in 1940. St. James was built on the north side of the railroad tracks on North H Street. Over the years, St. James was a particularly active parish. It was instrumental in the establishment of other parishes, schools, education programs, and social and legislative action for minorities.[15] By the 1990s, Catholics constituted the largest religious body in Las Vegas, accounting for over thirty percent of the total population.[16] Thanks to the growing Hispanic immigration after 1980, Las Vegas became the fastest-growing diocese in the nation by the 1990s.

The Presbyterians had a "shadow" presence in the valley as early as 1910. That is when their articles of incorporation were filed with Nevada Secretary of State, W. G. Douglas.[17] In 1912, the Las Vegas Age listed Presbyterian services under "church notices" and stated Reverend Jay Mortimer Swander was the pastor but did not print an address or service time.[18] Reverend Swander was the pastor of the Presbyterian Church at Rhyolite and may have posted the notice in hopes of pioneering a work in

13. George, "Stories of the Old West," 6.

14. Ibid.

15. Vincent, "James the Little Church with Many Seeds," 6.

16. Memorandum, (printed by the Diocese of Las Vegas, November 20, 2001). The diocese office provided a copy of the annual report sent to Rome. The report consisted of statistical information from 1995–2000.

17. Lowman, A Voice in the Desert, 13.

18. Las Vegas Age. Church Notices, September 14, 1912.

Las Vegas. There does not appear to have been a local active Presbyterian congregation until 1953 when Presbyterian records mention representation of the Las Vegas congregation at their annual presbytery meeting.[19]

The Mormon story once again became part of Las Vegas' development in 1912. In that year, Newell Leavitt moved to Las Vegas from Bunkerville, California, in search of work. Leavitt soon married, settled into a new home, and began a Sunday school in his house. Before long, he had a small Mormon congregation meeting in his home. There were no recognized Mormon wards in the valley, so the new work fell under the jurisdiction of Overton. Not until 1922 did church leaders design an independent branch in Las Vegas. (A branch is a congregation small in population.) It began with 149 members but quickly grew, prompting officials in Salt Lake to make the city a ward.[20] Local Mormons built their first chapel on the northwest corner of Sixth and Carson in 1925. Area growth continued, and by the end of 1930 as construction began on Hoover Dam, the church had over 400 members.

Thanks to the Hoover Dam project, Las Vegas' population soared to over 5,000 helping to boost the Mormon community to 500 members by 1932, and 825 just four years later.[21] Their structural foundation for growth included a plan for creating new stakes throughout the valley. The Las Vegas ward was divided first in 1941 and then again in 1947. The division of individual stakes did not slow the growth of the area-wide church. Church membership was determined geographically, thus residents of designated neighborhoods were expected to remain faithful to the ward closest to where they lived. Church growth was accomplished through the conversion of existing residents and new Mormon families moving to town. The first ward that had been cut into two in 1941 grew to 1,200 members by 1952.[22] The Mormons also established a training center for Mormon young people. While they called the center a seminary, it was not a seminary in the commonly understood sense of the term because it offered no formal degrees and was not an accredited institution. It did,

19. Lowman, A Voice in the Desert, 13.

20. Historical Department. A letter dated-March 10, 2000, from the Church of Jesus Christ of Latter Day Saints and signed by senior archivist Ronald G. Watt.

21. Earl, *The History of the Las Vegas First Ward*, (copy of Mr. Earl's typed history of the Mormons in Las Vegas), 3–14. Earl Marion came to Las Vegas in 1932. He was the first counselor of the First Ward and also served the LDS church as a counselor.

22. Ibid.

however, provide doctrinal instruction and extensive discipleship training that strengthened and extended the Mormon presence and enabled
students to engage in church missions.[23]

Another important factor in the Mormon success was its strong
financial base. For Mormons, tithing was not optional. Then, as today,
it was a requirement in order to enjoy membership in good standing.
Besides the tithe, fast offerings, offerings for the poor, and dues for the
maintenance of the ward were part of the expected donations. With a
solid financial base, expansion continued, and the Mormons eventually
became one of the strongest religious communities in Las Vegas. Their
millennial theology, evangelistic fervor, and organizational genius all
contributed to their success. The Mormon message held particular appeal
because of its emphasis upon socially conservative values, its help for the
poor and needy, a strong family emphasis, and good strategic planning.

Mormonism is a faith that is distinctly American in many ways
but nonetheless has traditionally been regarded as an outsider's religion.
Theologically, it stands outside the Protestant mainstream, but it proved
to be attractive despite its unorthodox theology. Its doctrinal idiosyncra-
sies were offset by messages addressing "felt needs." Mormons want to be
recognized as an expression of mainstream Christianity, so to this end,
they emphasize the practical application of faith rather than doctrinal
teachings.

Mormonism grew in the Las Vegas Valley along with the city. When
the sin industry began to evolve, it did not slow the growth or integration of Mormonism into the fabric of the local culture. Church rules
were modified to allow Mormons to work in certain aspects of the hotel
and gaming industries. Mormons also became an active force in local
business, banking, government, and education. By the 1940s, there was
a consensus among Latter Day Saints that in Las Vegas, gambling and
Mormonism were inextricably linked together.

Years later, Howard Hughes' posture towards Mormons exemplified the attitude of other local business leaders. He sought out Mormon
employees because he believed they could be trusted. There existed a
dialectical relationship between Sin City and Mormonism. The Mormons
provided integrity, skill, and a work ethic that was valuable in the bur-

---

23. David Rowberry. Interview by author, February 2000. Dr. Rowberry is the director of the Las Vegas Institute of Religion on the campus of UNLV.

geoning tourism industry, and the city's strong economy provided lucrative financial opportunities for many Mormon residents.[24]

The organized presence of the Baptists began in March 1923. The American Baptist Home Mission Society, with headquarters in the East, treated the American West as a mission.[25] Many of its new churches established in the region were built in railroad towns. The Baptists often sent a railroad car to a target town and used it as a temporary church facility until a permanent structure could be erected. On March 2, 1923, the Chapel Car "Grace" rolled into the desert community of Las Vegas.[26] Reverend E. P. Hermiston and his wife served as the first ministers. Following Pastor Hermiston's unexpected death a few months later, Reverend A. C. Blinzinger took charge of the enterprise.[27] In a little more than a year, he organized the First Baptist Church with fourteen charter members. They quickly began work on a permanent facility that was completed in March of 1925, and this building remained their home for the next twenty years. The congregation, however, grew slowly with a membership of only sixty-seven as late as 1944.[28] These numbers began to swell following the installation of Reverend Walter Bishop. Under his dynamic leadership, the congregation outgrew the old building and constructed a new one on the corner of Ninth and Bridger Streets.

One of the trademarks of First Baptist was its missionary-minded congregation. First Baptist members helped establish churches in North Las Vegas, Overton, Henderson, and later the West Charleston Baptist and Warm Springs Baptist churches.[29] The Baptists sponsored weekly Sunday schools at Blue Diamond, Goodsprings, Pahrump, and Goldfield. The congregation also established a Spanish-speaking Bible class for Hispanic residents in the northwest part of the city.[30] One former pastor of First Baptist remembered the spirit of cooperation that knit Baptists

24. Bradley, *Las Vegas and the Mormons*, (BBC video aired on television in the United States on 05/01/00).

25. *First Baptist Church. 50th Anniversary, 1924–1974*, 1–3.

26. *Las Vegas Age*. No author cited, "Baptist Chapel Car," March 3, 1923.

27. *First Baptist Church. 50th Anniversary, 1924–1974*, 1–3.

28. Ibid.

29. Malvin Pekral. Interview by author, December 1999. Rev. Pekral served as pastor of First Baptist from 1961–83.

30. *First Baptist Church. 50th Anniversary, 1924–1974*, 1–3.

together with other Protestant congregations in the city, and joint community services were well attended on Thanksgiving and Good Friday.[31]

The Christian faith of the valley's African-Americans was an especially important dimension of their life in Las Vegas. Blacks formed churches as soon as they arrived in town. There was not another section of Las Vegas that had more churches per square mile than the Westside. This constituted the epicenter of the African-American population. The first African-American church in Las Vegas was Zion Methodist organized in 1917. Up until that time, the town's few Methodist blacks wanted to have a church of their own but had to worship alongside the white Methodists at First Methodist Church. Members of First Methodist successfully petitioned the Union Pacific Railroad to donate a parcel of land for a church site at the northeast corner of Second and Ogden Streets. A 12-foot by 20-foot small frame building was erected, and it housed the city's first African-American congregation.[32] The new congregation still did not have their own pastor. The pastor of First Methodist provided oversight for both the white and black congregations until 1940 when the first full-time African-American pastor was appointed.[33]

Prior to World War II, Las Vegas' black population remained small. As late as 1940, the census recorded only 178 blacks in the city limits.[34] Zion Methodist fit for short periods of time. Zion Methodist's rise to prominence began in 1960 with the arrival of Reverend Marion Bennett. He recalled the first month's income as less than $40. Bennett brought solid academic credentials to the little congregation. He was a graduate of both Morris Brown College and Gammon Theological Seminary in Atlanta, Georgia. Under his leadership, the church grew, became self-supporting, and supported the struggle for civil rights.[35] He headed the local chapter of the NAACP from 1962–66. Zion Methodist developed a solid reputation and attracted many educated professionals as parishioners. For example, the congregation included in its membership David and Mable Hoggard. David was president of the local chapter of the NAACP

31. Melvin Pekral. Interview by author, December 1999.

32. Zion United Methodist Church. *78th Anniversary Celebration Brochure.*

33. Marian Bennett. Interview by author, February 1996. Rev. Bennett has been pastor of Zion Methodist since 1960.

34. U.S. Department of Commerce, Bureau of the Census, *Census of Population, 1920–1960.*

35. Marian Bennett. Interview by author, February 1996.

from 1955–59 and ran the Economic Opportunity Board from 1965–82 while his wife was a prominent educator who later had a school named in her honor.[36]

Early in 1927, a group of missionaries associated with the Pilgrim Church of Christ Holiness denomination, headquartered in Jackson, Mississippi, came to Las Vegas with the intention of establishing a new church. Led by B. F. Armstrong, their effort began with a home Bible study group, and by October of that year, a church appeared on the corner of Second and Stewart streets.[37] This was the second African-American congregation to be established in Las Vegas.

The signature doctrine of this church was its emphasis upon pious living. It was one of a number of denominations formed in the aftermath of the liberal fundamentalist church wars of the early years of the twentieth century. Pilgrim Church of Christ Holiness held to a strict view of biblical inerrancy and measured the quality of faith by pietistic behavior.

The Las Vegas congregation eventually moved to North D Street where it established itself as an integral part of the African-American Westside community. Pilgrim Church was never a particularly large congregation, with a membership that fluctuated between fifty and one hundred members, but it was well known and respected among the local citizens.[38] Reverend George Harris was the pastor with longest tenure. He served as Assistant Pastor from 1940–51 and then as Senior Pastor from 1953–71. The church was never as active on the political scene as Zion Methodist was but it did use the pulpit to support civil rights.

The congregation that would eventually become the largest of all the Westside churches did not organize until February, 1942, when a group of nine individuals met at the home of Brother and Sister H. R. Robinson on Jackson Street in Las Vegas to discuss the possibility of starting a Baptist church for African-Americans. Among the group were Reverend and Sister B. T. Mayfield.[39] Mayfield was chosen to be the pastor and the

---

36. David Hoggard. Interview by author, February 1996. Mr. Hoggard was a leader in the black community. He served as head of the local chapter of the NAACP from 1955–59 and was director of the Equal Opportunity Board from 1965–82. He was also an active member of Zion Methodist Church.

37. Donna Ship. Interview by author, December 2001. Mrs. Ship has been an active member of Pilgrim Church of Christ Holiness since the 1940s. Her father, Rev. George Harris, held a pastoral role at the church from 1940–71.

38. Ibid.

39. *Second Baptist Church. The History of Second Baptist Church*, 19.

name Second Baptist was selected because the name First Baptist was already taken by the town's white Baptist church. It was a common practice for black congregations of the same denomination to select the name "Second" to identify their churches.[40]

The small group of charter members purchased a parcel of land and collected enough money to acquire a 20-foot by 40-foot tent for $35. The fledgling congregation met there for about nine months, but the church began growing immediately and had to construct a permanent building to house the congregation. Money was raised for a concrete block structure by buying blocks on a weekly basis according to how much money came in via the Sunday offerings. Thus, the church was established under the leadership of Pastor Mayfield.[41]

Reverend V. C. Coleman assumed the pastorate of Second Baptist in 1949 and served for twenty-five years. In 1978, Reverend Willie Davis became the church's pastor. Under Davis's leadership, Second Baptist membership rolls more than doubled, Sunday attendance surpassed the one thousand mark, and the offerings tripled. In 1989, parishioners dedicated a large sanctuary with seating capacity of 1,600.

Second Baptist became an important community center on the Westside. Numerous local politicians came to the church during election years and national civil rights personalities were invited to speak from its pulpit.[42] Indeed, Reverend Jessie Jackson was one of the featured speakers at the dedication of the sanctuary completed in 1989.[43] Second Baptist church soon became a pillar of the African-American community.

The 1940s witnessed the first great influx of blacks to Las Vegas. Between 1940 and 1960, the black population increased from 178 to 9,649.[44] During World War II, many were defense workers at Basic Magnesium in Henderson. There were also a limited number of jobs available for blacks in the hotels and casinos downtown and on the emerging Strip. Not surprisingly, this led to the formation of several new Baptist congregations including Second Baptist, the largest black Baptist church in Las Vegas.

40. Willie Davis. Interview by author, February 1996. Pastor Davis has pastored Second Baptist Church since 1978.

41. *Second Baptist Church. The History of Second Baptist Church*, 19.

42. Willie Davis. Interview by author, February 1996.

43. *Second Baptist Church. The History of Second Baptist Church*, 41.

44. U.S. Department of Commerce, Bureau of the Census, Census of Population, 1920–1960.

The first black Pentecostal churches were also formed during the 1940s, an event that will be covered later.

The soaring black population triggered increased racial conflict. Indeed, local blacks often referred to Las Vegas as the "Mississippi of the West." They secured jobs as porters or maids but were not allowed to work on the floors of the casinos as dealers or cocktail waitresses. During the 1950s, when black entertainers such as Nat King Cole or Sammy Davis, Jr. performed locally, they could not stay in downtown hotels. Nat King Cole stayed in a trailer behind the Thunderbird Hotel and Sammy Davis Jr. lodged at the Moulin Rouge (the only black-operated casino in town).[45] Up until the 1960s, African-American residents of the Westside recall overt harassment when they strayed outside their neighborhood boundaries after dark. It was common for them to be pulled over by the police and interrogated about why they were in the wrong part of town.[46] Some local blacks still attribute this discrimination to the city's strong Mormon influence. Mormon theology held that blacks bore the mark of Cain and thus were a cursed race. Because of this, they were not allowed into the priesthood of the Mormon Church.[47]

Las Vegas' African-American ministers played a vital role in the struggle for civil rights. Beginning in 1964, the local chapter of the NAACP successfully fought to change some of the city and state's segregation laws.[48] The impetus for change came in the wake of a visit to Las Vegas by Reverend Martin Luther King in April 1964. He inspired a sense of mission and activism that brought a badly needed "cash transfusion." Local black churches spearheaded an attack on the city's segregation laws. Black ministers used the pulpit for rallying their congregations, and churches served as community centers for identifying the problem and formulating a plan of action.

Despite the troubles of being a black Las Vegan, there were advantages, too. Among the most important was that discrimination caused the black community to become close-knit and mutually supportive. The church was perhaps the single most important institution in the African-

45. Moehring, Resort City in the Sunbelt, 182–83.

46. James Rogers. Interview by author, February 1996. Rev. Rogers has pastored Greater New Jerusalem Baptist Church since 1984. He also served as head of the local chapter of the NAACP from 1996–2000.

47. David Hoggard. Interview by author, February 1996.

48. Martin Bennett. Interview by author, February 1996.

American community. Its purpose and function were multidimensional. Black Las Vegans, like their counterparts across the nation, were deeply religious and church served as the focal point for the practice of their faith and for community activism. Black churches were not simply spiritual centers. They addressed the political challenges faced by both church members and citizens of their minority community. The NAACP depended upon the church for leaders, for financial and moral support, and for a platform to articulate their agenda.[49] The church's enduring appeal to local African-Americans was evidenced by the fact that even though most blacks moved away from the Westside they continued to drive there for church. Their community of faith remained an important link between the individual black Christian and the black community at large.

There existed a sense of fraternity between members of the various black churches. Theological differences were never as divisive among blacks as they were in the white community. Pastors and congregations spanned the differences did not weaken their solidarity. Clearly, the creation of churches was an integral part of the community developmental process in Las Vegas. Churches provided spiritual orientation, community service, and a sense of identity for many among the local citizens. For minorities, they also provided a forum to express their frustration and seek solutions to white oppression.

49. David Hoggard. Interview by author, February 1996.

3

Brush Arbor Birthright

IT STARTED IN THE American heartland in the twilight of the nineteenth century. First hundreds, then thousands, then tens of thousands of Baptists and Methodists, with a sprinkling of Quakers, Mennonites, and Presbyterians, left their home churches and joined one of the great religious migrations of modern times. Some have labeled these spiritual sojourners radical evangelicals. They held in common the conviction that the only true gospel was "four-fold." It included personal salvation, Holy Ghost baptism, divine healing, and the imminent second coming of Jesus Christ.[1] Almost all who constituted this emerging movement rejected what they perceived as the drift into theological liberalism of mainstream Christian Protestant denominations. It was in this context that the modern Pentecostal movement was born, a movement that became the fastest growing expression of Christianity in the twentieth century. By the late 1990s, Pentecostals numbered over five hundred million. The sheer magnitude of the movement demanded it be taken seriously and evaluated in light of its far-reaching influence.[2]

For this discussion, Pentecostalism is considered within the larger context of historical Christianity, yet distinguished from other Protestant denominations. The movement's formal beginnings in North America date from the early twentieth century, but this Spirit-led tradition has deep roots that extend to the origins of Judeo-Christian faith, exhibiting a strong connection with this family tree. Indeed, this Spirit-led branch continues to grow both in this country and around the world.

---

1. Wacker, *Heaven Below*, 1.
2. Barrett, *World Christian Encyclopedia*, 6.

In *American Originals*, Paul Conkin identified a number of expressions of Christianity that bear a distinct "made in America label."[3] Pentecostalism was one of those expressions. As a working class expression of faith, it embodied many elements of the general American religious experience emphasizing the special place of America in God's master plan and importance of human freedom in forging one's own destiny. As one writer put it, "Deep down they seemed to know that they were, as President Lincoln had said of Americans generally, members of the almost-chosen people, and their country the almost-chosen land."[4] It was also a democratic-based faith in that the laymen and women of any given congregation shaped its formation of faith and charted its destiny.

Grant Wacker contended that the early Pentecostals were economically disenfranchised. They were the "honest poor" who occupied the lowest base of the work force. Their financial plight was compounded by their low social status. As one early Pentecostal put it, they were the "scum of society."[5] They were outsiders culturally as well. For them, the world to come held much greater promise than manifest earthly reality. They therefore lived in the shadow of

Christ's second coming, which they believed would deliver them from this world's troubles.

As in the rest of the nation and around the world, Pentecostals had a measurable impact in Las Vegas in the twentieth century. Although no one knows just when the first ones arrived, by the early 1920s there were at least a few Pentecostals in the Las Vegas Valley. The ensuing years saw the movement grow numerically and even become a national phenomena. In the years after World War II, Pentecostals became a significant part of southern Nevada's religious community. While groups like the Mormons and Catholics also grew quickly, theirs was mostly transfer growth consisting largely of existing members who moved to southern Nevada.[6]

Pentecostal growth, on the other hand, was comprised largely of new converts. Not only was the Pentecostals' numeric growth impressive, they also tapped into segments of the local population that were historically unchurched. Pentecostals attracted members from the gambling and

3. Conkin, *American Originals*, 276.

4. Wacker, *Heaven Below*, 239.

5. Ibid., 200.

6. Kevin McAuliffe. Interview by author, January 2000. Rev. McAuliffe has pastored Saint Elizabeth Ann Seton Church in Summerlin, Nevada, since July 1, 1997.

entertainment industries who were not previously associated with any form of organized religion. Local Pentecostals successfully accommodated themselves to the unique "sin city" culture. The 1960s marked the turning point for their growth in Las Vegas. From that decade on, they increased in numbers, influence, and acceptance by other Christian denominations.

Many new Pentecostal churches organized, but there was neither a centralized authority nor an official statement of faith binding them together. Each group staunchly retained its individual autonomy. However, there were common doctrinal beliefs linking them. Virtually all pledged allegiance to a message that included belief in the absolute authority of Scripture, holiness living (personal piety), baptism with the Holy Spirit, miracles, and Christ's imminent return to Earth.

In the decades after World War II, mainstream Protestantism declined even as evangelicalism grew.[7] Some demographic studies indicate that over thirty percent of Americans claimed to be evangelical as defined by a "born again" experience.[8] Pentecostalism was a form of evangelicalism, and throughout the latter half of the century, Pentecostalism remained an important component of the ongoing restructuring of religion in North America.[9]

Twentieth-century Pentecostalism is a recent expression of an ancient spiritual pathway to God. Some scholars identify this expression of faith as the "enthusiast tradition."[10] Its heritage can be traced to the ecstatic prophets of the Old Testament such as Elijah and Elisha. These were not literary prophets, but rather signs-and-wonders men of God. Their mark in ministry was defined by raising the dead and making axe heads float on water. They stood in contrast to the classical prophets like Isaiah and Jeremiah who conveyed the rational written word of God.[11]

During the formative years of Christianity, the believers at Corinth embodied the enthusiast spirit. In 1 Corinthians 13–14, the apostle Paul admonished the Pentecostals of his day. He warned them against the dangers of a faith that relied exclusively on ecstatic experience.[12] This

7. Wuthnow, *The Struggle for America's Soul*, 72.

8. Barna, *What Americans Believe*, 176–77.

9. Balmer, *Mine Eyes Have Seen the Glory*, 24–25.

10. Knox, *Enthusiasm*, 103.

11. Scott, The Relevance of the Prophets, 45–49.

12. Fee, *God's Empowering Presence*, 216–19.

charismatic tradition extended into the post-apostolic era with Christian worship that included prophecy, speaking in tongues, visions, and mystical encounters with the Divine.

For instance, Clement of Rome who died in AD 96 documented the prevalence of spiritual gifts within the church. Irenaeus of Lyons (AD 130–202) described charismatic gifts (especially prophecy) in his church in southern Gaul.[13] Also in the second century, a Phrygian evangelist named Montanus traveled throughout Asia Minor proclaiming himself to be the bearer of direct revelation from the Spirit of God. In trances, he believed he could reveal the direct word of God to the people of his day. The mystical Phrygian placed his private revelations on a par with Scripture.[14] One of the most respected early church fathers—a highly regarded theologian named Tertullian (AD 160–225)—eventually joined the Montanist "New Prophets" who practiced healing, prophecy, and tongues.[15]

During the early years of the Middle Ages, Simeon the New Theologian (AD 949–1022) was an Eastern mystic who reported intimate spiritual experiences. These included a "baptism in the Holy Spirit" which was distinct from those graces received in the sacraments. This Spirit baptism was accompanied by awareness of one's guilt before God, penitence, tears, and an intensified awareness of the Trinity as light dwelling within. Hildegard of Bingen (AD 1099–1178) professed to having aspired visions, gifts of tears, knowledge, wisdom and prophecy. Numerous miracles were attributed to her. She claimed to sing concerts in the Spirit and later legends maintained she wrote entire books in unknown languages.[16] The Cathars (AD 1100–1300) were regarded by the Catholic Church as heretics because they replaced the recognized sacraments with a belief in strict asceticism and "baptism with fire and the Holy Spirit."[17] Another western mystic named Gregorius Palamas (AD 1296–1359) emphasized the laying on of hands for reception of the gifts of healing, miracles, foreknowledge, wisdom, diverse tongues, and interpretation of tongues.[18]

13. Burgess, "The Pentecostal Tradition," 40–41.

14. Moynahan, *The Faith*, 115–17.

15. Burgess, "The Pentecostal Tradition," 40–41.

16. Ibid.

17. Peters, *Heresy and Authority in Medieval Europe*, 103–7.

18. Burgess, "The Pentecostal Tradition," 40–41.

The later Middle Ages had its representatives of the enthusiast tradition as well. Saint Francis of Assisi (AD 1182–1226) was the first to bear the stigmata. In ecstatic worship, the wounds of Christ appeared on his hands, feet, and side.[19] In addition, there were numerous references to mystical experiences among monks and nuns in the monasteries and convents. Saint Thomas Aquinas (AD 1227–74) spent most of his career developing a written systematic theology, but near the end of his life he claimed to have a direct revelation that rendered all his written work as nothing more than "wood, hay, and stubble." Aquinas professed to have experienced things that transcended the boundaries of his heretofore rational theology.

During the years of the Reformation, the Anabaptists were still another expression of Spirit-enthused faith. The radical reformers emphasized the priesthood of all believers, and taught that the spiritual gifts listed by the apostle Paul in 1 Corinthians 12 should be freely exercised by members of the congregation.[20] The charismata were a distinct feature of mainstream Anabaptism led by such men as Menno Simons and Conrad Grebe. Spirit directed religion was also a feature in the theology of a radical German Anabaptist named Thomas Müntzer (1490–1525). Müntzer, the eccentric Anabaptist was yet another example of the enthusiast tradition. He emphasized the "inner word" and baptism of the Holy Spirit and direct revelation through visions and dreams. He believed in Spirit guidance, and used his Spirit theology as a road map directing social reform.[21] Müntzer sought to usher in the kingdom of God on Earth by proclaiming Münster in Germany to be the New Jerusalem. At the point of the sword, he attempted to force the local citizenry to subscribe to his unorthodox theology. Many of the townspeople revolted and there was much bloodshed in a conflict between Münster and Müntzer. In the end, Müntzer and some of his followers were executed for leading the insurrection. Müntzer's violent apocalypticism earned him the nickname "Müntzer the monster of Münster." An interesting postscript to the millenarianism of Münster lies in the fact that he was lauded as a hero by some Marxists. They praised his militaristic interpretation of the kingdom of

---

19. House, *Francis of Assisi*, 258–63.

20. Friedmann, *The Theology of Anabaptism*, 29–32.

21. Williams, *The Radical Reformation*, 47–58.

God's arrival on Earth. They re-worked some of his ideas and folded them into their theory of class struggle inevitably leading to a utopian state.[22]

Between the years 1640–1801, the Jansenists were a French-based extreme Augustinian movement within the Roman Catholic Church. Among other doctrinal distinctives, they were also known for their emphasis upon signs and wonders, spiritual dancing, healings, and prophetic utterances. Some reportedly spoke in unknown tongues and understood foreign languages in which they were addressed.

Enthusiasm and American revivalism went hand in hand. The revivals and awakenings in American church history were punctuated by emotive faith. Jonathon Edwards (1703–58) noted tears, trembling, groans, loud outcries, religious "noise," and ecstasies during the First Great Awakening. Edwards himself first encountered God in an intensely experiential way while reading 1 Timothy. He later stated that the only language that seemed adequate was that of ecstasy. He was transfixed with "a sweet sense of the glorious majesty and grace of God that I know not how to express."[23]

There has always been a powerful experiential dimension to American revivalism. This reached a high-water mark in the famous Cain Ridge, Kentucky revival of 1800–1801. Over twenty-five thousand attended, and there were reports of ecstatic utterances, howling, and physical convulsions under the power of the Spirit of God.[24]

These historical examples are presented in support of the hypothesis that modern Pentecostalism is a contemporary expression of a long-standing Judeo-Christian tradition. Distinct from ritualists, who emphasize the sacraments, and rationalists, who emphasize the written and spoken word, are the enthusiasts, who stress the manifestation of the Spirit as an authoritative means to having an encounter with God.

The battle between modernists and traditionalists led indirectly to the formation of modern Pentecostalism. In the years following the Civil War, the face of American Protestantism was permanently changed. It was no longer a single theology, but divided into two separate camps. The long-held optimistic belief that America was a united Christian nation on

---

22. Cohn, *The Pursuit of the Millennium*, 250–51.

23. Kling, "Language of Ecstasy," 34.

24. Synan, *The Holiness-Pentecostal Tradition*, 11–14.

a mission to convert the world was shattered by the Civil War. Churches were divided between North and South.

Depending on one's theological orientation, either breakthroughs or breakdowns in scholarship challenged many of the traditional claims of Christian faith. As a result, a debate broke out between the creationists and evolutionists. Literary criticism challenged the veracity of many of Christianity's supernatural tenets of faith. Churchmen were divided on whether or not Jesus really performed miracles or was raised from the dead.

Another point of controversy was the modern school of psychology led by Sigmund Freud. He contended that the religious impulse in human kind was really nothing more than an infantile illusion rooted in the subconscious. All of these issues created spirited debate and eventually brought division within American Protestantism. The liberal churches sought to embrace the modern theories of thought and reconfigure Christianity to accommodate the new worldview. But millions of rank and file Protestants held their ground and would not budge concerning time-honored aspects of apostolic faith. The conservative camp, after the great division, came to be known as "fundamentalism." The term Fundamentalist was derived from the Presbyterian general assembly of 1910. In response to some of the questions raised about orthodox faith, the conference adopted a five-point declaration of "essential doctrines." These points were (1) the inerrancy of Scripture, (2) the virgin birth of Christ, (3) his substitutionary atonement, (4) his bodily resurrection, and (5) the authenticity of miracles.[25] A believer's position on these five points served as a litmus test for orthodoxy.

It was out of this movement that a new wave of revivals occurred. Among the holiness contingent within the fundamentalist confession of faith, there was fresh emphasis upon an experiential encounter with God and a firm commitment to the full authority of Scripture. Pentecostalism can be interpreted as a recent chapter in the longstanding enthusiast tradition of faith. Most Pentecostals' roots were in the Methodist and Baptist churches, although many detoured through the holiness movement in route to Pentecostalism.

Pentecostalism in America began in 1901. An obscure itinerate preacher named Charles Parham started a Bible school in Topeka, Kansas.

25. Marsden, *Fundamentalism*, 117.

The group, consisting of only a couple dozen men and women, met in an unfinished mansion the locals called Stone's Folly. Parham instructed his students to study the New Testament book of Acts. There was particular interest in the phenomena of the Holy Spirit in the life of the early Christians.[26] Parham's group was an independent collection of seekers who were not led by a scholar or committed to a particular theological tradition. In order to confirm that the experience of the early church was also intended for today, Parham encouraged his disciples to pray and ask God to duplicate the experience of speaking in an unknown tongue. A woman named Agnes Ozman was part of the group. Shortly after midnight on January 1, 1901, she spoke in an unknown language.[27] Parham and his followers believed this was the same experience of Spirit baptism that occurred in the early church. Soon the other members of the group had the same experience. Although Topeka Bible Institute floundered and soon closed its doors, the message of the baptism in the Holy Spirit as evidenced by speaking in other tongues lived on. The tiny but fervent Topeka contingent scattered and spread the word of their new revelation.[28]

What happened at Topeka might have passed without any further attention had it not been for a one-eyed black man named W. J. Seymour. While in Texas, Seymour heard Parham's fascinating teachings. He traveled to Los Angeles in 1906 and spoke one Sunday morning at a Nazarene church on Brae Street where he promised to teach more about the new doctrine of the Holy Spirit that night. However, upon returning in the evening, he found the church locked. Seymour rented a boarded-up livery stable on Azusa Street and began studying and praying, along with a small band of curious seekers, for the Pentecostal experience of the Holy Spirit. The result was the Azusa Street revival, a phenomenon lasting three years. Sparks from Azusa Street flew in every direction as the new faith spread with remarkable rapidity. Eventually, thousands came from across America and from other nations to be part of the Azusa Street revival. This revival ignited the modern Pentecostal movement.[29]

A descendent of the evangelical family, the Pentecostal movement emphasized the born-again experience and insisted upon full biblical

---

26. Menzies, *Anointed to Serve*, 34–39.

27. Blumhofer, *The Assemblies of God*, vol. I, 81–82.

28. Menzies, *Anointed to Serve*, 34–39.

29. Ibid., 41–48.

authority over matters of faith and practice. As with other forms of evangelicalism, the Bible was a key to Pentecostalism. Belief in the absolute accuracy of Scripture and its full authority over the believer in all matters distinguished them. Although the modern Pentecostal movement shared much in common with evangelicalism, it also had many differences. Pentecostals were distinguished by their emphasis on and devotion to studying the Holy Spirit.

Pentecostal eschatology was another distinctive characteristic. Historically, it fit into what H. Richard Niebuhr called the "Christ against culture" perspective of faith.[30] Since most early Pentecostals were drawn from the lower economic classes, they were not part of America's cultural mainstream. Lacking any optimistic faith in the secular world, they instead placed their trust in God. Pentecostals were characterized by their pre-millennial eschatology that anticipated the personal and eminent return of the Lord.[31]

Many of the twentieth century's first Pentecostals had their roots in the "holiness movement," placing a high priority upon personal piety. While not too concerned about broader social issues, they did emphasize personal holiness.[32] Smoking, drinking, gambling, dancing, and the like were always on the Pentecostal list of forbidden behaviors. They linked the ability to live a pious life to the internal habitation of the Holy Spirit. These "pneumatics" believed the Spirit's presence enabled one to overcome the temptations of the outside world. They interpreted society in general as lost and under the dominion of Satan. Separatism was also an important factor in living the "sanctified" life. They frowned upon relationships with people outside the community of faith who might entice indulgence in forbidden behavior. These beliefs stamped them as social separatists practicing their faith outside the boundaries of mainstream culture and placed them in an adversarial relationship with society in general.

One of the most common sermon topics was the second coming of Jesus Christ. The hope of Christ's return to earth was a dominant theme that resulted in members' prioritizing their lives based on the conviction that Jesus might return for his bride, the church, at any moment.

---

30. Niebuhr, *Christ and Culture*, 45–82.

31. Menzies, *Anointed to Serve*, 328–30.

32. Dayton, *Theological Roots of Pentecostalism*, 65–66.

This blessed hope made the miseries of earthly existence bearable. It also necessitated that one live in a constant state of alert. To be caught in a sinful state at the time of the Lord's return would mean being left behind to face the Great Tribulation. Every activity and ministry was geared to winning as many converts as possible before Christ's return. The end-of-the-world emphasis of the Pentecostals motivated them to be zealous evangelists seeking to spread the faith to anyone who would listen. They believed in and anticipated the end of the world once every nation on earth had received a witness to the Pentecostal version of the Christian faith. A favorite Scriptural text often cited in support of this position was Matthew 24:14, "And this gospel of the kingdom will be preached in the whole world as a testimony to all nations, and then the end will come." Pentecostals were relentless in their determination to convert as many as possible to trigger Christ's return.

Pentecostals had a distinct understanding of biblical authority. They held an abiding conviction that the Bible was infallible. They spoke of Scripture as the "all sufficient rule for faith and practice," but they did not evenly integrate the literal teachings of the Bible into the practices of everyday life. Some scholars believe this was because it never occurred to them to raise the question of what they meant by plenary accuracy.[33]

Pentecostals differed from fundamentalists concerning how biblical authority worked. While fundamentalists were strict literalists in that their interpretation of the biblical message was restricted to the context of the Bible itself, Pentecostals had a more "pneumatic" hermeneutic. They believed the Holy Spirit must be factored into the reading of Scripture. Pentecostals were not as bound to the letter of the text as they were open to the "Spirit" of it. For instance, a strict fundamentalist would adamantly oppose the ordination of women based on a literal reading of the New Testament, but Pentecostals have ordained women since the beginning of the movement. In fact, the most famous female evangelist in American history was a Pentecostal named Aimee Semple McPherson. Pentecostals reasoned that Paul's admonition concerning women in ministry was cultural, not a universal mandate.[34] To Pentecostals, the Spirit was more important than the letter in correctly applying the biblical message. These pneumatic Christians believed the Holy Spirit gave a sense of priority,

33. Wacker, *Heaven Below*, 73.

34. Poloma, *The Assemblies of God at the Crossroads*, 103–4.

emphasis, and timeliness to the test of Scripture. Scripture was absolutely authoritative as the Spirit spoke through it.

Also in contrast to fundamentalists, Pentecostals practiced a more energized, experiential form of worship which emphasized music and congregational participation. A possible influence for this was the spiritual tradition of the African slaves in the Old South.[35] Pentecostals embraced strong egalitarian ethics and were empowered by an active laity. Like Luther, they believed in the "priesthood of all believers" through which any member of the congregation might be used by the Holy Spirit to deliver the "Word of the Lord" to the rest of the church body. Pentecostals believed in divine healing as a sign or wonder and they made it central to their church's ministry. Nationally known ministries such as those of Aimee Semple McPherson, Oral Roberts, and Kathryn Kuhlman were built around faith healing.[36] Divine healing has remained a staple of Pentecostal faith and has been a cardinal point of divergence from many others within the evangelical community.

In its earliest days, Pentecostalism was distinguished by its racial inclusiveness. Blacks and whites worshiped side by side at the Azusa Street revival. The first African-American denomination, the Church of God in Christ, ordained a number of white ministerial candidates before fellowships like the Assemblies of God became organized.[37]

Today, however, the color line divides Pentecostals in several ways. It is no longer common to find integrated congregations. In some cases, upward mobility has separated the races. More whites than blacks have moved into the middle and upper middle economic classes. Whites who used to worship with the poor from all races now worship in well-appointed, predominately white middle-class churches in suburbia. Another reason for separation is worship style. Black Pentecostals are generally more exuberant in their worship than white Pentecostals. Sectionalism has been still another reason for the racial divide. Pentecostalism has been less capable of breaking down racial barriers in the South than other regions of the United States. There has also been a political division between Anglo and African-Americans. White Pentecostals have been political

---

35. Matthews, *Religion in the Old South*, 200–202.

36. Harrell, Oral Roberts: An American Life, 121.

37. Synan, *The Holiness-Pentecostal Tradition*, 71.

conservatives, often identifying with the ideology of the Republican Party, while a majority of black Pentecostals identify with the Democratic Party.

In *The Democratization of American Christianity*, Nathan Hatch demonstrated how populist and democratically oriented forms of Christianity both created new forms of Christianity and influenced the culture at large.[38] Pentecostals were consistent with Hatch's theory concerning democratically oriented American expressions of faith. Pentecostals have been an upwardly mobile movement rapidly finding their way into the American mainstream socially, economically, politically, and religiously. The proliferation of Pentecostalism exerted a visible impact on American culture in the twentieth century by attracting members or supporters from all social classes in American society.

While twenty-first century America is much more religiously pluralistic, it will probably also be decidedly more evangelical/Pentecostal. Princeton sociologist Walter Wuthnow is convinced that a re-structuring of religious allegiance and influence is currently underway. He maintains that expressions of evangelicalism including Pentecostalism are emerging as the new religion of the American mainstream.[39]

The days of retreat from mainline culture are over, as the pentecostal community asserts itself in politics, education, legislation, and social activism. In the present, on any given Sunday, there are more Pentecostals in houses of worship than Presbyterians and Episcopalians combined. There was a time when Pentecostal worshipers were few in number and came from the margins of society.[40] Now there are not only millions of them, but they are moving into professions and stations in society that have a shaping influence upon the course of the nation's culture. Former United States Attorney General John Ashcroft is a lifelong member of the Assemblies of God, as is former Alaska governor and vice-presdential candidate Sarah Palin. Oscar-winning actor Denzel Washington and basketball legend Magic Johnson are members of a Pentecostal, Church of God in Christ, congregation in Los Angeles. Pentecostals are becoming a strong conservative voice in the national dialogue over social issues such as the right to life movement and gay marriage.

---

38. Hatch, *The Democratization of American Christianity*, 3–9.
39. Wuthnow, *The Restructuring of American Religion*, 173–83.
40. Anderson, *Vision of the Disinherited the Making of Americanism*, 100–101.

An element of Pentecostal genius is their ability to re-invent elements of their message to fit into a new cultural context. Examples of this, during the decade of the 1980s, were televangelists Jim Bakker and Jimmy Swaggart. They were masters at packaging their message in an attractive popular format. This theme is effectively surveyed in Laurence Moore's *Selling God*. He argues that the principles of a free market even apply in the ecclesiastical context. Moore shows that those religious groups that understand the market and make their movement relevant to the needs of the common people have always been rewarded with success.[41]

In a post-modern world, the foundations of cultural, intellectual, and spiritual absolutes have all been challenged. Harvard scholar Harvey Cox studied the Pentecostal phenomenon on a worldwide scale and concluded that it was the Pentecostal understanding of Spirit that helped spur their rise to prominence. Pentecostals are not anti-intellectual but they are pro-Spirit.[42] For the Pentecostal, Spirit has entered the arena as a legitimate means for people to define and reinterpret truth. Pentecostalism has expanded far beyond its American origins and has become a powerful international movement especially in Latin America.[43] For millions, the Spirit has become the new absolute.

By the year 2000, Pentecostals claimed over 500 million followers world-wide with tens of millions in the United States alone.[44] Pentecostalism cuts across all ethnic and cultural barriers. In the United States virtually every ethnic group boasts Pentecostal congregations. For example, the Church of God in Christ is the largest African-American Pentecostal denomination. By 2000, it boasted a worldwide membership of ten million.[45] Hispanics, Koreans, and Filipinos also joined Pentecostal churches in impressive numbers.

Indigenous churches have been established on every continent around the world. For example, the church is rapidly growing in parts of Africa. In Nigeria, Pentecostalism grew from less than 1 percent of the total population in 1900 to over 32 percent by the year 2000.[46] In Asia it

---

41. Moore, *Selling God*, 267–76.

42. Cox, *Fire From Heaven*, 300–301.

43. Ibid., 177.

44. Barrett, World Christian Encyclopedia, 6.

45. Ibid., 5.

46. Ibid., 549.

is growing as well. The *World Christian Encyclopedia* identified Yoido Full Gospel Church in Seoul, South Korea, as the largest single congregation in the world. In 2000, this Assemblies of God church had a membership of 900 thousand people.[47] It is impossible to accurately count the number of Pentecostals in communist China, but two things are evident: first, there are more of them now than when the communist revolution began, and second, the Chinese church has a strong Pentecostal component. David Barrett estimates there are over 54 million Chinese pentecostals.[48] Approximately 47 percent of the Christians in Brazil are now Pentecostal/ Charismatic. In the 1990s, Russian Orthodox Church prelates spoke out against Pentecostals, a sure sign of their emerging presence in that country. Conservative estimates today put the number of Russian Pentecostals at nearly 6.5 million.[49] India, a predominately Hindu country, has also seen an explosion of growth among Pentecostals. Many converts to Pentecostal Christianity come from the lowest castes of society. Christianity offered hope for self-improvement while Hinduism left the lowest members of society immobilized by their karma. From 1970–2000, Pentecostals in India increased by over 30 million.[50] Harvey Cox believes their influence is even beginning to make inroads into Western Europe and speculates the growth will continue.[51] There is no indication Pentecostal growth is slowing at all, as it continues to increase in size and influence as a world-wide religious movement. The Las Vegas Pentecostal experience has followed much the same path from its humble beginnings, inclusion of all races, political influence, promotion of women, acceptance into mainstream culture, and rapid growth.

47. Ibid., 684.
48. Ibid., 191.
49. Ibid., 624.
50. Ibid., 360.
51. Cox, *Fire From Heaven*, 211.

4

Pentecost in Their Souls

WOMEN HAVE ALWAYS PLAYED a prominent role in Pentecostal churches, and Las Vegas was no exception. In virtually every Pentecostal congregation, women comprised the numerical majority and usually shouldered a heavy load in leading the practical ministries and spiritual life of the church. This chapter will use the example of one local woman and congregation to illuminate the role of women in the Holy Spirit centered religion's development and growth.

The story of Pentecostal women zigzags. In some instances, they served as missionaries, teachers, and even pastors. The Old Testament book of Joel was often quoted, "Your sons and daughters will prophecy" (Joel 2:28). This passage was interpreted as biblical endorsement for women in leadership. On the other hand, some Pentecostals were uncomfortable with women at the helm, because the apostle Paul expressly forbade them from holding a position of leadership over men (1 Tim 2:11–12).

The issue of women in leadership depended upon how one interpreted the authority of Spirit and Word. Did the direct revelation of the Holy Spirit commission women to take the lead, or was the written authority of Scripture to be followed to the letter? Pentecostalism existed with this ambiguity unresolved.[1]

Emma Jacobsen's life provides an excellent case study, because she embodied so many characteristics that typified the Pentecostal movement. She came from a working-class background and was a spiritual leader in both her home and her church. She was a fervent believer in the contemporary ministry of the Holy Spirit, and was a strict separatist

---

1. Wacker, *Heaven Below*, 166.

from the prevailing Las Vegas culture. Jacobsen remained a vanguard for the old-time religion when Trinity Temple began moving away from its classical Pentecostal roots and began recasting its image and message to better relate to a new generation of believers. As a Los Angeles resident, she was baptized with the Holy Spirit in the early twentieth century. The Azusa Street revival introduced her to the Pentecostal experience. Her experience of speaking in other tongues alienated her from denominational churches, so she joined a small Pentecostal fellowship. While in Los Angeles, she attended a crusade and came under the influence of a rising star on the evangelistic trail, Aimee Semple McPherson.[2] Sister Aimee was both an inspiration and an example of a Pentecostal woman in the ministry. In established Protestant churches, it was unacceptable for a woman to take the lead in pulpit ministry; not so with Pentecostals. From the movement's beginning, women were recognized as potential pastors and ministers in their own right.

Because Pentecostals were egalitarian in the practice of their worship and interpreted themselves as a priesthood of believers, this meant any Spirit-filled believer in the flock could be a conduit through which the Holy Spirit might be manifest. The congregation did not rely on the pastor to be the Spirit's exclusive mouthpiece. Jacobsen believed the Lord had given her the gifts of discernment and prophecy. She thought the exercise of her spiritual gifts was her way of ministering for the good of the entire local body of believers. It was not unusual for her to bring a "message in tongues" during a Sunday service. On other occasions, she gave "the interpretation" when someone else spoke in a heavenly language. At times she possessed the "gift of discernment" When this occurred, she sensed if something was out of order or inappropriate and would go to the pastor or church elders to make her feelings known.

In 1931, Emma Jacobson's family moved to Las Vegas. Her husband, Carl, had the promise of work at Boulder Dam, so he packed his belongings, loaded his wife and their three children into the car and headed east from Los Angeles. Making ends meet had always been a struggle for Carl, and these were hard times. Carl blamed the stock market crash of 1929 and the depression for his family's economic woes. Yet as recounted by his daughter, Ellenore, Carl himself was part of the problem. He was mentally unstable, had outbursts of anger, and was later diagnosed

---

2. Ellenore Nighswonger. Interview by author, October 1992. Mrs. Nighswonger became a member of Trinity in 1931. She is the daughter of Emma Jacobson.

as schizophrenic. Being married to him was not easy. More than once Emma was the target of physical abuse. There were times the children were compelled to intercede on their mother's behalf. Sometimes they had to physically pull Carl away from Emma. The Jacobsons had high hopes for a better life when they moved to Las Vegas. Carl purchased a lot at 800 Williams Street, and the family lived in a tent at the end of the lot. For the next few months, the family worked together constructing a house using materials left over from the Hoover Dam project. Soon after moving to town, Emma went door-to-door selling corsets while Carl started a junkyard business near their property in North Las Vegas. The family needed the extra income from outside jobs to supplement Carl's paycheck.[3]

"Sister" Jacobsen's faith was an important part of her life. Las Vegas was a lonely place for a morally upright woman like her, and she found strength, help, support, and inspiration from the practice of her Pentecostal faith. Perhaps her frustrations and disappointments at home were also part of the reason the Lord was so important to her. Mr. Jacobsen once was an active churchman himself, and for a period of time he and his wife had even co-pastored a church. But that was in the past. Carl had long since quit practicing his faith and did little to encourage his family in religious matters. Emma's faith was probably the glue that held her unstable marriage together. She believed that the Bible strictly forbade divorce; so her marriage to Carl never hinged on whether, but how, it would work out. As it turned out, it did not work out very well at all. She never divorced him, but she did pack his belongings and permanently banish him from her home. Religion helped console and strengthen her as a single parent. Church was vital because it provided a place for worship and fellowship with others who shared her values.[4]

From the time Mrs. Jacobsen arrived in town, she began looking for a Pentecostal fellowship. Her choices were limited, because Pentecostals were a tiny, obscure minority in Las Vegas in the 1930s. In the terminology of the outside world, she was a "holy-roller." The first organized church she attended in Las Vegas was Zion Rest Mission. Zion Rest was a small predominately black congregation (see chapter 5). She later heard

---

3. Ibid.

4. Ibid.

about Westside Mission and, with her two youngest children, decided to give it a try.

At the Westside Mission, Jacobsen found what she was looking for. Church services were held at least three times a week, and she was present whenever the doors were opened for worship.[5] On Sunday mornings in the early 1930s, Mrs. Jacobsen, her daughter Ellenore, and son Burt walked about four miles to Westside church. Their destination was a rickety, unpainted structure with only a wood-burning stove providing heat in the winter. There was no running water, and they sat on wooden benches that had neither backs nor padding. The pastor's labor was one of love for there was no salary to support him. While he took a percentage of the offering, that usually amounted to only four dollars per week.[6]

Jacobsen's newfound Pentecostal church had only about twenty-five members. Sunday morning's church experience began with Sunday school. She taught an adult Bible class. She felt that since the Bible contained the blueprint for successful living, it was important to spend time studying its contents. After Sunday school, the morning worship service was held, which began with energized singing. The music was usually upbeat with some of the saints clapping their hands or tapping their toe to the beat. During one period, the pastor's daughter played the piano and danced while she played.[7] After the song service, members of the congregation were encouraged to stand and testify about how the Lord had answered prayer or helped them through the past week. It was often the pastor's wife who led the song and testimony service. Occasionally, she brought the Sunday morning message.[8] After the closing prayer, Jacobsen and her children visited with their friends and hoped one that of the members would invite them home for Sunday dinner. Visiting with Christian friends over a meal on Sunday afternoon was a treat they looked forward to. There was never much socializing associated with church attendance. When congregants came together to worship, they were to focus on spiritual matters. However, a close social network developed between families who were part of the congregation. The Pentecostals'

5. Ibid.

6. Brenda Arnold. Interview by author, April 1992. Mrs. Arnold attended Westside Church (later Trinity Temple) in 1940.

7. Ibid.

8. Ellenore Nighswonger. Interview by author, October 1992. Mrs. Nighswonger became a member of Trinity in 1931. She is the daughter of Emma Jacobson.

separatist theology kept them at arm's length from unbelievers, and this rejection of the general society caused them to draw together with others who shared the faith. Their homes were opened to one another for meals, leisure, and helpful support in times of need.[9]

As Mrs. Jacobsen surveyed the congregation, she saw dozens of poor working class people who were dressed in their Sunday best. The men wore shirts and ties and the women wore dresses. It was unacceptable for women to wear slacks in public. Makeup, jewelry, and lipstick were also against the rules. No one had the smell of alcohol or tobacco on their breath, because drinking and smoking were strictly forbidden.[10] To be sure, there was probably a sipping saint or two, but this censored activity was kept a closely guarded secret. Pentecostals taught that such transgressions might be enough to cost one their salvation. Most of the adult church members were employed. Virtually everyone had to work hard just to get by. Sam Willitts was a retired carpenter and Neal McGarvey was a plumber. Brother Jeeters worked as a supply manager for a public school. One woman served as a file clerk for Basic Magnesium while Helen Swett toiled in the dry cleaning business. They labored outside the home, not because they chose to be career women, but because a cash shortage forced them to seek outside employment.[11] There were no statistical studies done to determine the percentage of women who worked outside the home, but interviews with members from the period indicated most of the women in the congregation had to work in order to supplement household income.[12]

The Westside Mission was led by a Latino pastor named Francisco Moreno. "Brother" Moreno was a poor man with a wife and two children and had to work a secular job to support his household. Financial help from the church consisted of a weekly free-will offering, which was usually less than ten dollars.[13] There were not many Latinos in Las Vegas in the late 1920s and 1930s. In fact, they numbered less than one percent of

9. Ibid.

10. Ibid.

11. Ibid.

12. Ibid.

13. Brenda Arnold. Interview by author, April 1992. Mrs. Arnold attended Westside Church (later Trinity Temple) in 1940.

the population until the 1960s. The 1960 census registered 236 Hispanics within the city limits amongst a total population of 64,405.[14]

When Emma Jacobsen came to the Westside church, she found a small but racially diverse congregation. There were some blacks, whites, a Japanese family, and a few people of Mexican descent. Among the Mexican contingent was the Rodriguez family. Albert and his wife, Jessie, came to Las Vegas because Albert got a railroad job. Albert Rodriguez arrived as a young man who did not have the benefit of a formal education, but his work ethic and desire to succeed was evidenced by the fact that he taught himself to read and write English. For years, Albert's family was the only Rodriguez listed in the Las Vegas phone book.[15] Like Emma Jacobsen, Jessie was the spiritual leader of her home. She and her children began attending the Westside Mission at the invitation of an unnamed Hispanic lady who was part of the fellowship. It was important to Jessie that her family retain their Spanish heritage, but she and Albert also believed it essential that their children assimilate into the culture of their adopted homeland. Jessie was fully involved in the ministries of the congregation, and her family helped build the benches that provided seating.[16]

From 1928 to 1939, the nucleus of the Westside congregation met in several locations and was led by four different pastors. It was in 1939 that the congregation built a permanent facility on 10th Street and affiliated with the Assemblies of God. Then on August 29, 1946, Helen Swett filed a Certificate of Incorporation with the state of Nevada to officially rename the church Trinity Assembly of God. By this time, the congregation had grown to include approximately 200 members.[17]

Mrs. Jacobsen never gave much thought to getting involved in social or political issues because she believed they were part of the lost cause of the existing non-believing world order. Her hope was invested in the coming of the Lord. She believed that only when Christ returned would an upside-down world be righted. Most of her friends were in the church. She was polite and cordial to outsiders, but her closest associations were

14. U.S. Department of Commerce, Bureau of the Census, *Census of Population, 1910–1980.*

15. David Rodriguez. Interview by author, October 2002. Mr. Rodriguez is the son of Albert and Jessie Rodriguez.

16. Lupe Morgan. Interview by author, October 2002. Mrs. Morgan is the daughter of Albert and Jessie Rodriguez.

17. *Fiftieth Anniversary*, (printed by Trinity Temple, 1989), 4–5.

with those who shared her faith. She looked forward to the monthly meeting of the Women's Missionary Council. The church women established this organization to support the cause of world missions. They raised money and collected food, clothing, and household items that were sent to missionaries serving abroad. The monthly meeting not only provided an opportunity to do the Lord's work, but also to enjoy friendship of other women of faith.

One missionary the church supported was a single woman from Wisconsin, Hilda Wagenknecht, who had sailed to India in 1920. She felt the call to full-time ministry as a teenager. She had once been engaged, but her fiancé did not share her passion for missions. Rather than forsake her calling, she forsook the mores of her culture to be a wife and mother and sailed to Bettiah, India, alone. Once there, she single-handedly established an orphanage and school for young girls. Wagenknecht went without guaranteed salary, depending solely upon volunteer support from churches in Arnerica.[18] Jacobsen and the other ladies in the church provided her with some financial support and packed barrels with material goods they had made or collected. These were sent to help sustain the orphanage. Years later, Hilda Wagenknecht moved to Las Vegas and became Trinity Temple's record keeper and taught a Bible study.

In some ways Pentecostal women like Emma Jacobson were pioneers and in other ways quite accepting of the status quo. They were among the first women to be involved in virtually every ministry of the church. In subtle ways they demonstrated strength and assertiveness. The Lord was their ultimate master and even husbands had to take a back seat. Whether or not Carl approved, Mrs. Jacobsen practiced her faith and developed a social life centering on the church. In other ways, she was not as independent minded. Her other-worldliness nurtured ambivalence towards social issues. Whereas women of other faiths had been social activists, Pentecostal women were not so inclined even during the Great Depression and World War II.

Jacobson was uncomfortable when a new pastor came in 1954. Pastor Cecil Robeck joined the ministerial association and his wife, Berdette, became an active member of the Las Vegas Minister's Wives Fellowship. The church, then named Trinity Temple, began moving away from its classical Pentecostal roots and commenced recasting its image and message to

18. Hilda Wagenknecht. Interview by author, April 1992. Rev. Wagenknecht was Trinity's record keeper from 1975–1998.

better fit the mainstream culture of Las Vegas. Here, Mrs. Jacobsen feared the wall separating the church and the world was eroding. An uneasy relationship existed between Jacobsen and the Robecks; the Robecks even suspected Jacobsen had a hand in their ultimate dismissal.[19] The Robecks stayed in town after their termination and opened another church, but relations between the Robecks and Emma Jacobsen were permanently strained.

In 1958, Reverend Wilbur Wacker came to lead the flock. The church had grown numerically to include over 250 people. The new pastor had more impressive credentials than his predecessors. He was college educated and had served as a representative of the Billy Graham Evangelistic Association.[20] Whether or not Mrs. Jacobsen liked it, Trinity was rapidly becoming part of middle America. Jacobsen was representative of the old guard Pentecostal who looked with suspicion at any move towards assimilation with popular culture. However, there were other members who were more receptive to broadening the base of the Pentecostal tradition to reach a more diverse constituency.

There were increasing numbers of middle-class families attending, so the congregation relocated, and in 1969 built a new sanctuary that could potentially seat 875 people. The new church building was located at 1000 East St. Louis. The move to this location planted the congregation in a more upper middle class part of town. As a result, the church began attracting a higher socio-economic group of people. There was a sprinkling of professionals among the congregants where it had previously been solidly blue collar. The children of some of the charter members were now adults. Some of them had a better education than their parents, and most of them held good-paying jobs. This dramatic change in the class status and location of the church was the basis of a major turning point in Trinity's identity and the definition of what it meant to be Pentecostal in Las Vegas. The local Pentecostal holy-rollers were becoming socially acceptable.

One element of classical Pentecostal faith that did not change was its eschatology. Trinity's members remained staunch in a belief that they were living in the last days. The military threat of the atheistic Soviet Union, the reestablishment of Israel in the Jews' ancient homeland,

19. Cecil and Berdetta Robeck. Interview by author, April 1994. Cecil Robeck served as pastor of Trinity from 1954–56.

20. *Fiftieth Anniversary*, 12.

and the international outpouring of the Holy Spirit, were all perceived as startling fulfillments of prophetic passages of the Bible. Pentecostals in Las Vegas, as everywhere, else lived in anticipation of Christ's second coming. Upward mobility, the tension between separatism and cultural assimilation, and last day's fervor were factors that defined the emerging Pentecostalism of Las Vegas. Many of the old timers like Emma Jacobson were still part of the church, but the epicenter was shifting.

A new kind of parishioner was now joining the church, one which mixed religion with Las Vegas' somewhat unique lifestyle. Kay Brown visited Trinity for the first time in 1966. A woman of Brown's background would never have fit into the old Westside church. She had been a professional entertainer since she was a little girl. Although baptized a Baptist when just twelve years old, she had been infatuated with life in the fast lane as a Hollywood entertainer, and as a result, she had forsaken her spiritual moorings. Brown became a "backslider." She was an actress and a singer who had won acclaim, but something was missing in her life. Her professional life was a resounding success, but her personal life was in disarray. By the time she was thirty-two years old she had been married six times and was searching for something that would bring order and fulfillment to her life. At Trinity she found a vibrant congregation that met her needs. The preacher's message promised the possibility of a personal relationship with Jesus Christ. A strong experiential faith was just what Brown needed to reassemble the broken pieces of her life.[21] Emma Jacobsen was from poor working class stock; Kay Wood came from a lifestyle of affluence and prestige. Emma was plain and undecorated, while Kay was a walking fashion statement. Kay Brown was not typical of the new kind of Trinity adherent, but she represented a new breed of convert who would not have felt welcomed in the past.

By the time Brown came to Trinity, it was a respected, well-attended church. Women were becoming more actively involved in many aspects of the church's ministries. It was common for women to lead in congregational singing and worship. The Women's Missionary Council was active. One of its projects was to make bandages for an overseas leper colony. Women also sewed material goods for needy people, especially other believers who were in want. Council members were always ready to prepare meals for families in an emergency situation. Whenever there was a

---

21. Kay Wood. Interview by author, April 1992. Mrs. Wood was a professional singer until coming to Trinity in the 1960s.

special building project, they worked in construction right alongside the men.[22]

Grandma (Emma) Jacobson was an elderly woman by this time but was still prominent in the church. She was one of a group of older ladies who were active in a fervent prayer ministry. One lady in the group, Sister Norris, claimed she could not read anything except the Bible. She credited the Holy Spirit with giving her the ability to read God's work, but that was all she could read. The ladies' prayer group spent time every week interceding for the church's needs. If the women knew someone was struggling, they paid them a visit in an effort to help them.[23]

It was still common for some of the women of Trinity to work outside the home, but the cult of domesticity was becoming more popular. A higher economic standard of living enabled more women to concentrate exclusively on their roles as homemakers. Trinity never taught against women in the workplace, but it did prioritize the woman's role of wife and mother as her highest calling. A woman's place in church leadership was also changing. In the earlier days, women often preached, but that was now rare. In the past, women had served on the church board, but that did not happen anymore.[24] Numerical growth and upward mobility had brought more men into the congregation and elevated their position. In the past, women often ministered because there was a shortage of men, but this changed once the church attracted more men. Trinity continued to grow and became one of the city's larger congregations. In the mid-1960s, weekly attendance stayed close to four hundred, and the congregation was now solidly middle class. There were a number of teachers, business people, and other white-collar professionals sprinkled among this working class church. Moreover, Trinity saw the arrival of the first individuals employed in the gambling industry.[25]

A more upwardly-mobile congregation and a beautiful state-of-the-art sanctuary in a desirable neighborhood demonstrate that a new generation of Pentecostals embraced certain forms of materialism. Pastor Wilbur Wacker was more open-minded than his predecessors, and he

22. Vita Souza. Interview by author, September 1992. Mrs. Souza was active at Trinity since the early 1950s. She was Women's Ministries director during the 1960s.

23. Ibid.

24. Cecil and Berdetta Robeck. Interview by author, April 1994.

25. Vita Souza. Interview by author, September 1992. Mrs. Souza was active at Trinity since the early 1950s. She was Women's Ministries director during the 1960s.

broke with past patterns in a number of ways. For one thing, his wife, Shirley, was always fashionably dressed and liked to wear cosmetics and jewelry. This was in stark contrast to the earlier generation of Pentecostals who branded all such emphasis upon outward adornment as sinful and worldly. Maybe the Wackers' "worldly dress" was one reason why more mainstream middle-class people felt comfortable in the church. However, this new permissiveness paradigm opened the door to other problems. There were at least two sexual affairs involving prominent church members. Some older members were alarmed by the new ways and believed a spirit of worldliness had entered the church. The old Pentecostal holiness codes may have held certain outward behaviors in check with its emphasis upon unadorned simplicity and separation from the world. Some of the members interpreted the new ways as accommodation with the world and believed it contributed to a climate that encouraged temptation and sinful behavior inside the church.

The most turbulent period of Trinity's history occurred in the early 1970s. A pastor with a charismatic personality, Reverend Bill Sharp, came and wooed the people with his flamboyance. "Reverend Sharp" and his wife, Nancy, had a colorful background. He was a former prizefighter and made the unsubstantiated claim that he was once President Harry Truman's bodyguard. His wife, Nancy, was an attractive woman, a fashionable dresser, and a talented musician. She took over the role as choir director, and she was an accomplished soloist. Her musical talents were both entertaining and spiritually uplifting. The boundary between the church and entertainment on the Strip was becoming more blurred than ever before. Nancy was active behind the scene working with women's ministries, but she was not a pulpiteer. She came from a wealthy family, and her husband sometimes tapped her financial resources to finance his personal agenda. Once he even commented, "I checked to make sure she really had money before I married her."[26] The Sharps brought a high profile to Trinity. They moved the congregation even further away from its pietistic roots of the 1930s and 1940s.

At first, members greeted the Sharps with excitement and enthusiasm. They brought a flash and style that was foreign to traditional holiness-minded Pentecostals. Pastor Sharp's dashing appearance and machismo captured the attention of some of the women. Nancy's fashion-conscious

26. Ibid.

image encouraged other churchwomen to make themselves over in a stylish manner. Sharp was also a spellbinding orator who convinced many to respond to his public invitations to accept Christ as savior. Aggregate weekly attendance now exceeded 1,000 people. The growth of the congregation and the number of decisions for Christ seemed to legitimize the new brand of Pentecostalism. It was no coincidence that the church's growth coincided with an increase in Las Vegas' population. Between 1970 and 1980, the city grew by approximately forty thousand people.[27] It appears that the church's growth partly reflected the city's growth.

The Sharps were infatuated with the sparkle of Las Vegas and enjoyed identifying with Strip entertainers such as the McGuire sisters and Robert Goulet.[28] They published a magazine highlighting their ministry in the city and spread the word about what "God was doing in Vegas."[29] Most of the claims turned out to be exaggerated, but Sharp was a master promoter and knew how to draw the public's attention. He was not concerned with separation from the world but sought instead to give, church approval to the entertainment industry and reconcile the church and the Strip. By early 1974, allegations and rumors about the pastor's sexual misconduct and misuse of church finances began to circulate within the church and in the Las Vegas community in general. Nancy Sharp was respected by all, but rumors of Bill's misconduct persisted and created a widening rift over the controversy. Emma Jacobson was among those who suspected something was wrong, and she went to a church board member to tell him.[30] The last year of Sharp's tenure was fraught with accusations of immorality and misuse of church funds. The charges were later substantiated by a woman who will remain anonymous. She was the victim of a sting operation when another female friend arranged for two board members to listen in on a phone conversation in which she acknowledged a sexual affair with Pastor Sharp. Suspicions of financial corruption were substantiated when official bank records, produced by a board member named Eldon Grauberger, showed checks made out to

---

27. U.S. Department of Commerce, Bureau of the Census, *Census of Population, 1910–1980.*

28. *New Dimensions Magazine*, published by Rev. Bill Sharp during his years as pastor of Trinity Temple.

29. Tell, *"Trinity's Envoy of Light and Life."*

30. Ellenore Nighswonger. Interview by author, October 1992.

Trinity Temple had been cashed by Pastor Sharp for personal use.[31] A number of the women in the church were personally attracted to Pastor Sharp, but their infatuation turned to revulsion when they learned of his philandering. The reaction of his wife through the ordeal was interesting. Nancy remained calm and collected. Never did she show any sign of slackening loyalty to her husband. The ordeal of the Sharp years rocked the congregation to its foundation. Pastor Sharp left in 1974 as an angry and unrepentant man. He took about two hundred church members with him and started an independent ministry. They first met in the casinos and later purchased a theater which they converted into a church. A more detailed account of the tumultuous Sharp years will be found in chapter 6 entitled Revival on the Strip. In the fall of 1974, Reverend Melvin Steward and his wife, Norma, came to the helm at Trinity. Their years at Trinity were marked by exceptional congregational growth, expansion of ministries, and the establishment of a grade school. Pastor Steward was an evangelist at heart. His passion was winning converts. The primary mission of the church was once again evangelism.[32] Mrs. Steward was quietly active in the ministries of the church. She taught the Young-Married's Sunday School Class, led W.M.s (Women's Ministries) and was an accompanist on the piano or organ. Norma enjoyed being involved at the church, but her highest priority was supporting her husband and maintaining their home.[33] Attendance at Trinity mushroomed to a weekly average in excess of two thousand, plus thousands more who were on the church rolls.[34] Sunday services were broadcast throughout Nevada, parts of California, Utah, and Arizona. Trinity began an aggressive program of church founding. Between 1977 and 1982, the congregation was instrumental in the establishment of Assemblies of God churches in the southern Nevada towns of Tonopah, Overton, Pahrump, Alamo, and Henderson. Trinity also established a church in the eastern portion of Las Vegas and came

31. Eldon Grauberger. Interview by author, September and October 1994. Personal diary,

January 1974. Mr. Grauberger served as a board member of Trinity during Bill Sharp's pastorate.

32. Melvin and Norma Steward. Interview by author, October 1994 and January 2002. Rev. Steward pastored Trinity from 1974–84.

33. Ibid.

34. Hilda Wagenknecht. Interview by author, April 1992. Rev. Wagenknecht was Trinity's record keeper from 1975–98.

to the rescue of two local struggling Assembly of God congregations, Mountain View Assembly and Faith Assembly of God Church.[35]

New ideas took shape at a revitalized Trinity Temple. In 1975, "Adams Rib," a new expression of women's ministry was formed, and catered to the interests and needs of younger female members.[36] Reports of their activities included helping needy families with food and clothing, special seminars focusing on self- improvement topics, and Bible study sessions. Marriage and family were also important topics. Some subjects used to be taken for granted, but life in the 1970s brought new challenges to the nuclear family. In response, the church developed special ministries to bolster the traditional concept of marriage and family.[37]

It was the young women at Trinity during the 1970s who began paying special attention to social issues. They were concerned about public school curriculum, sexual mores, pornography, abortion, and drug abuse. Although there was an emerging interest in the abortion issue, there was no record of church members being involved in any organized effort against it until 1984. A social consciousness developed at Trinity in this decade. While the pulpit ministry of Trinity was a factor, Pastor Steward was more interested in personal conversions than social activism, although he encouraged his congregation to vote and speak out on some of the moral issues of the time. Matters of particular concern included divorce, sexual promiscuity, and the sanctity of human life.

Under his stewardship, the church became active in supporting local Christian media. In 1972, KILA Christian radio began broadcasting in Las Vegas. It was immediately popular among the women of Trinity. From the radio station's inception, Trinity Temple was a strong financial supporter. The church also provided equipment to carry broadcasts throughout the southwest.[38] In return, KILA broadcast Trinity's Sunday morning worship services. Based on mail the station received, station owner Jack French believed the audience consisted mostly of women. Thus, KILA's morning program schedule catered especially to them. This practice has remained constant since the station opened.[39] "Focus on the Family" was among

35. Melvin and Norma Steward. Interview by author, October 1994 and January 2002.

36. Vita Souza. Interview by author, September 1992.

37. Ibid.

38. Ibid.

39. Jack French. Interview by author, March 1992. Mr. French is owner and manager of KILA Christian radio station established in Las Vegas in July 1972.

the most popular programs aired. The broadcast featured Dr. James Dobson, a licensed psychologist in California and an Associate Professor of Pediatrics at the University of Southern California from 1969 through 1983. Presidents Carter and Reagan both appointed Dr. Dobson to serve on various White House task forces. His program consistently centered on social issues important to Pentecostal women. These issues included prayer in public schools, pornography, abortion, and the preservation of traditional nuclear families.

In the late 1970s, Trinity operated a small bookstore. No records remain from the period, but conversation with the woman who operated it revealed that Bibles, Dobson publications, and Christian self-help books sold best.[40] This was consistent with best-selling items at Christian bookstores. It is safe to conclude that conservative Christian publications also fed the emerging social agenda of local Pentecostals. Trinity's records during the years 1982–84 show that it contributed more than $175,000 annually for world missions but only $300 one time to Crisis Pregnancy Center.[41] CPC. was an organization dedicated to finding alternatives to abortion. Financial records clearly demonstrated that social activism did not displace evangelism in the financial commitment of the church. Still, women comprised an important segment of the church, and in a sexually liberated town like Las Vegas, proper female behavior was a major concern. An examination of several Mother's Day sermons reveal Pastor Steward's position concerning the role of women in the church. Never was there criticism of women working outside the home, nor were there any messages criticizing women in the ministry. One sermon was based on the Old Testament text of Proverbs 31 and centered on the requirements of being a Christian mother. The points included devotion to one's husband, love for home life and children, modesty in dress, praise for the Lord, and being a credit to her family. This sermon was quite typical and expressed the church's beliefs concerning Christian womanhood.[42]

Another sermon entitled "Modern Mothers" stood out. It did not prescribe home and hearth as the only acceptable role for a Christian

---

40. Melvin and Norma Steward. Interview by author, October 1994 and January 2002.

41. *Trinity Temple Annual Report, 1984*, 22. This was the year the Nybakkens came to pastor Trinity. There is no record of CPC support before they came.

42. Steward, "A Good Mother—A Bible Definition," Mother's Day message preached by Rev. Steward at Trinity on May 11, 1975; "Modern Mothers," Mother's Day message preached by Rev. Steward at Trinity on May 13, 1984.

woman. But it did distinguish between Godly and ungodly femininity.[43] Presumably, this left the door open to new definitions of womanhood within a biblical context. The message idealized motherhood as a woman's highest calling, but it did not have anything to say about women who remained childless or who were career oriented. A review of other sermons revealed the same basic emphasis of God and family as the top priorities.

Pastor Steward's popularity and moral teachings drew an impressive influx of new converts during his ministry. Records reveal that 2,666 individuals signed conversion decision cards between the years 1974–84.[44] Some of the conversions were unorthodox and typically "Las Vegas" in nature. In the mid-1970s, a Lido dancer named Allison came forward to make a profession of faith. A Lido dancer's attire consisted of a few strategically placed rhinestones and an ostrich feather headdress. This was hardly acceptable dress for a standard Pentecostal woman! Not only did Allison want to join the church, but she brought two other dancers who also expressed an interest in membership. A short time later, they submitted applications to the church board, which ignited a serious discussion regarding whether or not women from the Strip met the church's criteria for membership. Finally, one board member broke the ice and spoke persuasively on behalf of the women. He said if he "was going to err, he would rather it was on the side of grace than on the side of legalism."[45] He made a motion to accept them as members, the motion passed, and the women were accepted as official members. These women all expressed a desire to start new careers once their employment contract expired, and in the course of time, they did.

This episode is revealing. First, we catch a glimpse of one reason women were attracted to Trinity. The call for a "born again" experience held promise for those caught up in a way of life they wished to escape. A new beginning appealed to those who were disappointed with their life situation. In some instances, it was a broken marriage, for others it was addiction to gambling or alcohol. The list goes on, but the common denominator was an opportunity to break out of a lifestyle that they wished to escape. Also informative is the church board's response. When Emma Jacobson was a young woman, it was unthinkable for anyone involved

43. Ibid.

44. Hilda Wagenknecht. Interview by author, April 1992. Rev. Wagenknecht was Trinity's record keeper from 1975–98.

45. Melvin and Norma Steward. Interview by author, October 1994 and January 2002.

in such a "worldly" lifestyle to be part of the church. They might have accepted Allison if she made a

clean break with her dancing career, but they never would have accepted her as long as she continued in show business. The thinking of the church changed dramatically between the early years and the 1970s. Pentecostal pragmatism was certainly a factor. The church developed a more accepting definition of divine grace that invited even exotic dancers from the Strip to join the church.

The influx of newcomers brought women who had experienced a divorce. The church welcomed them, but for a time, some of the women might have felt out of place because the church's activities catered primarily to the traditional family. The church responded to the newcomers' particular needs by creating specialized ministries dealing with divorce, single parenting, remarriage, and blended families. One such ministry was the Fellowship of Christian Adult Singles (FOCAS).

Flexibility and innovation kept the church responsive to changing needs. Most of the extended ministries were led by laypeople. Trinity was democratically organized and thus was largely defined by the interests and involvement of the congregation. Women's ministries, a girls' scouting program, a day care center, and an elementary school were created in direct response to specific needs. A review of women's ministries activities provides insight into their priorities and interests. Bible studies were the most common activity. Topics included the work of the Holy Spirit in the life of a believer and the biblically-correct role of a Christian woman in the home, the church, and community. Women's prayer groups and missionary support were also

emphasized. Annual reports revealed the women were able to raise anywhere from five thousand to ten thousand dollars in any given year.

Even though no woman had participated in Trinity's preaching ministry since the 1950s, acceptance of women in the pulpit was still intact. Trinity sponsored a new congregation beginning in 1979 and appointed a woman to serve as pastor. This satellite church was the East Las Vegas Assembly of God. Reverend Evelyn Tyler, a widow, pastored it until her death in 1994. Her leadership emphasized children's programs and eventually took on the responsibility of serving meals to the homeless.[46]

46. Evelyn Tyler. Interview by author, May 1992. Rev. Tyler pastored East Las Vegas Assembly of God from 1977 until her death in 1993.

Trinity women were especially concerned about children's education. Various women served as head of Trinity's pre-school and daycare center. Others taught in the grade school, and three women were among the eight members of the school board. Special speakers came to address the women about involvement in public schools, encouraging mothers to take an active interest in what was taught in the classroom. There was concern about modern cultural trends, including the banning of school prayer, atheistic evolution, liberalized views of human sexuality, and moral relativism.[47] While many families kept their children in public schools, a significant number elected to home-school their children or enroll them in the church's private school.

Pastor Steward enjoyed much success with his emphasis on families, the role of women, and concern about secular education, but in time he and his wife looked to move on. In 1984, the Stewards left Trinity to accept another pastorate. Reverend Vernon and Betty Nybakken were chosen to take their place. This brought a change for the women's ministries. Pastor Vernon Nybakken was a mild mannered man, and his wife was an action-oriented initiator. Many remember Mrs. Nybakken as a more assertive leader than her husband. She led women's ministries and built a great deal of enthusiasm. She also had a passion for social reform and the rights of the unborn in particular. Crisis Pregnancy Center became one of her special interests. Largely through her initiative, CPC gained regular financial support from Trinity.

The church also encouraged members of the congregation to participate in right-to-life demonstrations. The Nybakkens personally participated in marches and made Trinity available as the geographical starting point. It was the first time on record that Trinity's pastoral leadership participated in a social protest.[48] Many older members had not, because it went against the grain of their separatist roots. The younger members, however, were more inclined to activism.

Registration of voters took place in the church foyer in 1988. This, too, was a first. Historically, pastors had encouraged church members to exercise their right to vote, but never before had registration been an organized effort. The pastor did not tell people who to vote for, but his fondness

47. Colleen Abbey. Interview by author, April 1992. Mrs. Abbey became a member of Trinity in the early 1960s. She was active in various ministries of the church and served as Women's Ministries director in 1990.

48. Ibid.

for Ronald Reagan was apparent. From the pulpit, he would sometimes refer to him as "Brother Reagan."[49] When the controversial movie "The Last Temptation of Christ" came to town, members of the church were encouraged to picket the theater where it showed. Pentecostal Christians believed the movie portrayed Christ in a sacrilegious manner. The congregation encouraged social activism after the Nybakkens came and it became a permanent dimension of the church. In 1990, the Nybakkens left Trinity. Some of the passion for social action left with them, but abortion was the single issue that remained a call to arms, perhaps because so much national attention remained focused on this controversy. Political concern remained on the agenda, but it did not displace the spiritual emphasis of Trinity's women. A review of the 1989 women's ministries handbook revealed the primary focus remained Bible studies, prayer meetings, missions, and benevolence. There were also specialized efforts to provide support groups for women without partners and address the particular needs of working women.

It should not be assumed that female members in the 1980s were radically different from their predecessors. Throughout Trinity's history, women shared a deep-seated piety. Every generation submitted to biblical authority, lived in anticipation of Christ's second coming, cherished marriage and family, and all believed women had a place in the ministry. There was one important difference, however: the women of the 1930s and 1940s were strict separatists while those living in the 1970s and 1980s were actively involved in cultural transformation,

Some have misunderstood America's Pentecostal Christians, considering them ignorant, backward, and out of step with the mainline culture of modern America. They have failed to recognize an entirely different stream of consciousness that claimed the loyalty of millions of middle class Americans. The women of Trinity were not eccentric extremists nor were they out of touch with reality. Many had good jobs, were financially secure and well educated. Trinity's women were one of a major block of people who were fundamentally religious in their world view. Their faith was not a crutch, but the foundation of their identity. Their beliefs concerning God, marriage, family, and the sanctity of human life were highly valued. They believed in traditional values and moral absolutes. Many of converts were trying to rebuild their broken lives. A significant number

---

49. Ibid.

of women became members of Trinity in the midst of domestic strife. Others were looking to put down roots in Las Vegas after moving there from other parts of the country. Personal transformation and belief in the world to come were the objectives of their faith. Although the viability and integrity of their way of life was not always appreciated, their devotion to Scripture, their emphasis upon prayer, their willingness to give sacrificially to world missions, and belief that they were living in the last days demonstrated that these women had strong and distinct convictions.

As literally thousands of Trinity converts migrated to other Las Vegas churches, the Pentecostal spark of the 1930s fanned into a flame. Emma Jacobson died in 1973, but her faith was born anew in the hearts of many local women. Pentecostals were no longer just a faint voice in the desert, but an influential force in an emerging city.

5

Coming into Holiness

HARVEY COX'S BOOK, *FIRE From Heaven*, analyzed Pentecostalism's impressive growth and surprising diversity. What Cox discovered on an international level also characterized the African-American segment of the local religious community. Black Pentecostals were an important ingredient in the local town-making recipe. Their spirituality created both a sense of identity and community. The story of African-American Pentecostals in Las Vegas was in many ways typical of the larger pattern of Pentecostal expansion.

Pentecostalism was not just an Anglo expression of faith. In Las Vegas' Westside, "Spirit filled" African-Americans were building congregations of their own. In the early years there were at least two integrated congregations, but later the color-line separated whites and blacks. African-American Pentecostals started out with strict holiness codes forbidding contact with the Strip. With the passage of time this practice changed. The black churches that flourished reworked their message so congregants could practice their faith yet still be involved in certain aspects of the entertainment industry. There were at least two important differences in style and function that distinguished their churches. Black Pentecostalism incorporated a distinct style of preaching, frequency of church attendance, and Africanized music and worship. Another distinction was the role of the church as an active component within the larger African-American community. They were not cordoned off from involvement in social and political matters as were their white counterparts. This is their story.

On November 11, 1941, a train made its regularly scheduled stop at the depot in Las Vegas. Clyde Carson Cox and his wife, Thelma, (affectionately called Sweetie) stepped off the train and set foot onto the soil of their new desert home. At that time, Las Vegas was a small isolated community. Prior to their move to Las Vegas, Cox and his wife pastored a number of churches in Iowa and California, with Oakland, California, being his most recent place of ministry. Las Vegas must have seemed a stark contrast to the mild climate in the Bay Area. Popular lore has it that C. C. Cox came at the behest of a prophecy, "this desert shall bloom as a rose." Las Vegas turned out to be his final and most fruitful place of ministry. The Cox's influence on the city was reflected by the fact that years later, in 1966, The National Worker's Guild of the Churches of God in Christ named Cox "The Man of the Year in Las Vegas."[1] Another testimony to his legacy was that almost twenty years after his death in 1969, an elementary school was named for him.[2]

In the early 1940s, there were less than three hundred blacks in the desert community of about eight thousand inhabitants. West Las Vegas was where the town's African-Americans moved after the city's white leadership herded them there in response to complaints about too much integration from southern Hoover Dam workers and tourists. In the 1940s, the Westside's boundaries ran from A Street to H Street North to South and Bonanza to Miller on the East and West. This part of town lacked many of the amenities that white Las Vegans in other parts of the valley took for granted. For instance, most of the streets on the Westside were not paved and most buildings did not have running water or indoor plumbing. One long-time West Las Vegas resident recalled there was only one well in his part of town, and it had to service all the residents.[3]

In those days, Las Vegas was a racially segregated town. Examples of blatant discrimination included the fact that black high school students were not allowed to participate in organized school activities. Their only involvement was as spectators. Nor could blacks be served in many local restaurants. African-Americans met at the Blue Onion, Blackies hamburger stand, or Phil's Drive-in and were served outside of these establishments.[4] In a typical example, Louise Miller and her sister Lois

1. *Jubilee Celebration 1948–1998*, 24.

2. School. *Clyde C. Cox Elementary, Dedication, Open House* (Program brochure, February 5, 1988).

3. Carruth Hall. Interview by author, February 2000. Bishop Hall has been active in the Church of God in Christ since the early 1950s. He has served as pastor of Greater Saint Paul Church of God in Christ since 1964 and has been bishop over the State of Nevada since 1993.

4. Ethel Cox. Interview by author, October 2000. Mrs. Cox was a long-time member

were invited to attend a meeting of the Southern Nevada University's student council leadership at Phil's Drive-in in 1955. When Louise and Lois tried to enter the restaurant, they were told to remain outside. The rest of the council members left the restaurant in protest.[5]

Segregation only reinforced the Westside blacks' strong sense of fraternity. During the 1940s, there was a grudging acceptance of discrimination. "It was just the way things were," commented one resident who lived in West Las Vegas during that decade.[6] Even with discrimination in Las Vegas, another resident commented, "Life was easier here than in the South."[7]

In 1940, the only two well-established, predominately black Protestant churches in the Westside area were Zion Methodist and Pilgrim Church of Christ Holiness. African-American Baptists had not yet organized a congregation of their own; Second Baptist was not established until 1942.[8] Black Pentecostals were few in number and not part of any established denomination in West Las Vegas. Some among this fractional minority worshiped at the independent Westside church or at Zion Rest Mission. There were other churches on the Westside, but they were racially mixed congregations. There was a Foursquare church at the corner of Washington and B Streets. Its members included whites, blacks, and hispanics.[9] There was also St. James Catholic Church, which consisted of a few Mexicans, Indians, whites, and blacks.[10]

---

of the Cox's Upper Room Church of God in Christ. She was also sister-in-law to Bishop C. C. Cox.

5. Louise Miller. Interview by author, September 2000. Ms. Miller moved to Las Vegas as a young girl in 1943. She has been a member of Cox's Upper Room/Pentecostal Temple since that time. She has served in numerous leadership capacities in the church including Sunday School teacher, president of the youth group, usher, choir member, and head of the Deaconess Board.

6. Ibid.

7. Francis Harris. Interview by author, August and September 2000. Mrs. Harris has lived in Las Vegas since 1942. Her husband was pastor of Prayer Church of God in Christ from 1961–70.

8. Second Baptist Church. *The History of Second Baptist Church*, 19.

9. Teresa Miller. Interview by author, December 2001. Ms. Miller's father, Bud Higgenbotham, pastored the Las Vegas Four Square Church from 1951–70. She has been a member of her father's churches since moving to Las Vegas as a child.

10. Bill Vincent. "St. James, the Little Church With Many Seeds."

Before the arrival of Reverend and Mrs. Cox, there were two black Pentecostal groups that would later support the Cox's ministry. One was a loosely organized group under the leadership of a man known as Elder Finley; the other was a small fellowship organized under Dad (Bill) Russell and his wife Mother Josie. Russell dabbled in real estate and purchased parcels of land in the valley. He was therefore able to provide a lot on F Street for a church building upon which he built a small cardboard structure. Named Zion Rest Mission, this served as the church home for a tiny congregation. It had a brush roof, was heated with a wood-burning stove during the winter months, and had unpadded chairs for seating. Cox inherited this cardboard church and a congregation of only six people. He re-named the church The Upper Room. Cox soon affiliated the congregation with the Church of God in Christ denomination.

Black Pentecostalism in Las Vegas centered around Clyde Carson Cox. He was a rarity among his Las Vegas African-American contemporaries in that he held earned college degrees. His bachelor's degree was from Moorehouse College and his PhD. from Trinity Hall College. Cox was a large man, standing over six feet tall and weighing well in excess of two hundred pounds, but he was a gentle, caring giant who tended to the practical needs of his congregation. He served, for instance, as a volunteer mail carrier. Twice a day he walked across town to the post office to pick up the mail and deliver it to his neighbors in West Las Vegas. This part of town lacked running water, so Pastor Cox regularly delivered water to the homes of those who were without. When the opportunity to obtain running water finally presented itself, Cox helped lay the water lines extending into West Las Vegas. It is said that on many occasions he reached into his pocket to provide financial help for individuals in distress. These and many other acts of kindness and community concern contributed to an enduring legacy.

Theologically, Cox believed the gospel had both a practical and spiritual dimension. It was a natural expression of his faith to respond to the everyday needs of people in the neighborhood. Cox was himself a man of limited personal financial resources, yet he did not work any outside job and relied solely on the contributions of church members to support him and his family. Evangelism was still another dimension to his ministry. From time to time he traveled outside the city to hold crusades, and donations from this activity supplemented his income.[11] Cox was an ordained

11. Louise Miller. Interview by author, September 2000.

minister with the Church of God in Christ. This predominantly black denomination was born out of the Azusa Street revival of 1906. Bishop Charles Harrison Mason was the head of the denomination headquartered in Memphis, Tennessee. The Church of God in Christ originally included both white and black members and clergy, but by the early 1940s, it was almost exclusively black. The color line among Pentecostals in Las Vegas was evident, as the Assemblies of God church (Trinity Assembly of God) was solidly white while the Upper Room Church of God in Christ remained exclusively black.

One theological characteristic that defined the Church of God in Christ was its doctrine of the Holy Spirit. Like all other Pentecostal groups, church members emphasized the manifestation of the Spirit in the life of present-day Christians. The infilling of the Spirit was evidenced by glossolalia (speaking in an unknown tongue under the influence of the Spirit). Another signature teaching was its "holiness" doctrine. To be a true believer meant one had to abstain from practices such as dancing, drinking, smoking, and a host of other personal behaviors considered sinful. In addition, one was not to frequent or work at establishments that condoned such a lifestyle. Church of God in Christ theology taught that the infilling of the Holy Spirit empowered the believer to overcome such indulgences. These Pentecostals also believed miracles still occurred in the present, and spiritual gifts such as prophecy and divine healing were contemporary ministries in the church.[12] The biblical passages used to define this aspect of their belief were 1 Corinthians 12 and Romans 12.

The Church of God in Christ grew in Las Vegas under the able ministry of Reverend Cox. Some new members were fresh converts to Christianity; others left denominational black churches and joined the Church of God in Christ, but most were newcomers who moved to Las Vegas, usually from the South. During World War II the opportunity for better jobs lured African-Americans to the resort city and Henderson's Basic Magnesium plant. With over thirteen thousand jobs at the factory and hundreds more in the bourgeoning resort industry, Las Vegas was a beckoning destination for many southern blacks, but it often still required two incomes to support a family. For this reason, it was common for wives and mothers to enter the workforce along with their husbands. To be sure, during the 1940s and 1950s, high-paying jobs were closed

---

12. *Annual Homecoming*, 1.

to blacks. They were not permitted to work in public areas of the hotels. Waiters, cocktail waitresses, and front desk jobs were unavailable to them. Even Hoover Dam, a depression-era public works project, hired only a smattering of black workers. Although blacks were restricted in the workplace, the available menial jobs paid better than those they formerly held in other parts of the country. Many worked as porters, others provided kitchen help, and a few worked at the hospital on 8th Street as well as defense jobs in Henderson.

For most black newcomers an important part of their incorporation into a new community included finding a church home. The church represented a buffer insulating the faithful from a sinful world, and easing the sting of racism in the segregated Las Vegas of the 1940s and 1950s. The community of faith has been an important part of African-American culture since the days of slavery. In the antebellum South, one of the few places slaves could gather in openness, free from the presence or listening ears of the master, was their place of worship.[13] The church became a forum for free expression, African styled worship, and the exchange of information and concerns which affected their daily life together. The Christian message also provided a catalyst for their hope. In times of oppression, their hope focused on the spiritualized kingdom of God, but their hope also became a vision for a better life in the secular world. The church as a faith-based community thus became a permanent dimension of African-American culture.

The community of faith was certainly an integral part of the Pentecostal subculture in Las Vegas. In 1942, the cardboard Upper Room Church of God in Christ was replaced with a brick structure constructed at the same location. In just one year the burgeoning congregation outgrew the brick building, and it was enlarged again in 1948.[14] In that same year, Elder Cox became a bishop charged with overseeing all Church of God congregations in Nevada.

Church involvement was an every-day staple of black life best evidenced by a steady diet of church attendance, sometimes seven days a week. When asked why they went to church so often, one charter member responded, "there was nothing else to do."[15] Undoubtedly, the church

13. Genovese, *Roll Jordon Roll*, 236.

14. *Annual Homecoming*, 50.

15. Group Discussion. Interview by author, August 2000. This discussion group consisted of five women who have been longtime members of the local church of God in

enhanced community life because it knit together minority residents in a town known among its black residents as the Mississippi of the West. For Pentecostals, the Christian faith also provided a beacon of hope with its message of the supernatural establishment of the kingdom of God on earth. A central tenet of faith was the second coming of Jesus Christ. Thus, belief in a new heaven and earth offset present frustration with life as an oppressed minority. Eschatology was an important component of African-Americans' faith. They lived their lives and practiced their faith in the shadow of the anticipated return of Christ.

Sunday was the focal point of the week. Despite the desert heat, all who attended church dressed in their Sunday best. One member who attended the Upper Room in those days commented that this had been the pattern "ever since slave times." Dressing up was one way of giving their best for Jesus on the Lord's Day.[16] The Lord's Day began with Sunday school at 9:45 a.m. The bishop taught the adults in a session that would last up to three hours. There was no organized children's program; therefore, children sat on the hard chairs with their parents and fidgeted during the long Sunday school session. Cox was an able Bible teacher, so the protracted study time focused on biblical instruction and exhortation. Sometime between 12:00p.m. and 1:00 p.m., the main worship service began. It always included an extended time of personal testimony and worship in song. There was not an organized song service, but as individual congregants felt led, one would begin a song spontaneously and the rest of the congregation would join in singing. Originally, there was only a piano to accompany worship in music, but later the tambourine and guitar were added. Eventually, drums became part of the musical ensemble.[17] The blend between testimonials and singing would go on for about an hour, although nothing was forced into or limited by a rigid time schedule. The timing, order, and sequence of the service were dictated by the "moving of the Spirit."

The signature belief of Pentecostals was that the "Holy Ghost" was expected to spontaneously move when believers gathered for worship. It was not uncommon for a congregant to speak out in another language (a message in tongues) and someone else to offer an interpretation of the

---

Christ. Their names are Georgette Franklin, Francis Harris, Ethel Cox, Louise Miller, and Alberta Davis.

16. Louise Miller. Interview by author, September 2000.

17. Ibid.

Spirit-inspired word from God. This frequently happened during the tes-
timonial time. Testimonies, singing, and the expression of spiritual gifts
were all a vital part of the worship experience.

The main Sunday morning worship service included prayer, collection of money offerings, and a biblically based message. The range
of sermon topics was somewhat limited. Messages on salvation, divine
healing, Spirit baptism, or the expected second coming of Christ were
the most common.[18] The preaching style of Bishop Cox was described
as "jubilistic." Jubilistic preaching was characteristic of black ministers.
It referred to an impassioned and energized delivery of the message.
Jubilistic preaching was rhythmic in delivery and elicited a congregational response while the message was being preached. The feel and style
of preaching was as important as the historical context. Bishop Cox's use
of Scripture was Pentecostal in character. His preaching exemplified the
pneumatic hermeneutic characteristic of Pentecostal exegesis. He was not
as concerned with the historical critical implications of the text as he was
about its existential relevance to the lives of his parishioners.[19] For Cox,
the Bible was a living document requiring the Holy Spirit to apply its
meaning and relevance for the church's congregation. Cox certainly drew
on insights gained from his theological training, but much of his preaching and teaching were best described as extemporaneous.

The church service would continue until sometime between three
and four in the afternoon. When it ended, members would go home for
dinner, but returned by 6:00 p.m. to attend the evening service. There
was great emphasis placed on the "altar service." This was an informal
time of prayer usually at the conclusion of the organized time of worship.
Members would pray together around the front of the humble sanctuary
seeking a fresh move of the Spirit. It was not uncommon for the evening
service to last until midnight. Often members held a "tarrying" service
when they gathered around the altar and prayed with a new member to
receive the infilling of the Holy Ghost as evidenced by speaking in other
tongues.[20] Members were free to leave whenever they wanted, but many
would stay as they drew strength and inspiration from time spent in
corporate worship. When asked about why they spent so many hours in

18. Ibid.

19. Cox tapes, Mother's Day 1967 and February 1969. These tapes of Bishop Cox's
sermons belong to Mrs. Ethel Cox, sister-in-law to the late Bishop C. C. Cox.

20. Louise Miller. Interview by author, September 2000.

church on Sunday, the response was "It's the Lord's Day." Apparently, rest and leisure were not considered worthy pursuits on Sunday. It was to be a day set aside to concentrate on worship and church attendance.

Church was not just a Sunday affair for members of Upper Room Church of God in Christ. Sometimes Monday would be a free night (unless there was a revival) with no services or activities scheduled, but during the rest of the weeknights the church was open. Tuesday was for corporate Bible study and prayer; Wednesday was youth night; Thursday evenings were set aside for more Bible study and evangelism; Friday was dedicated for a time of pastoral instruction and guidance; and Saturday evenings Sweetie Cox led choir rehearsal.

It was clear that Pentecostal community life centered on church involvement. Bishop Cox was revered as the congregation's shepherd, but volunteerism and lay involvement was extensive. Members of Upper Room formed a tight community consisting of "Spirit-filled" Westside believers. The Pentecostal emphasis upon the Holy Ghost and personal holiness set them apart from members of other Westside churches. The Upper Room became firmly established, and there were approximately fifty members by the mid 1940s. At least three factors promoted the church's growth. First, there were new converts. These were individuals who got "saved." To be saved meant to profess an experience of faith in Jesus Christ. Second, there were those who crossed over from other churches in West Las Vegas. Finally, there were many who joined the church after moving to Las Vegas from other parts of the country.

The term used to describe those who joined the Pentecostal church was "coming into holiness." The holiness codes provided structure and boundaries for some individuals who might otherwise have been vulnerable to excessive compulsive behaviors. For others, the motivation was that they could receive God's blessing by following the biblical blueprint for living. Smoking, drinking, gambling, and participation in organized sports activities were among the behaviors considered worldly and inappropriate. Sports, it was believed, could too easily become an idol. It was even unacceptable for young people to play marbles.[21] Cox did not want his church members to have contact with anything associated with gambling. Coming into holiness meant one forsook participation in all such activities. In some respects, it was easier for blacks to live the

21. Ibid.

holiness life in Las Vegas during the 1940s and 1950s, because they were not allowed to participate in the fledgling "sin" industry, which later became the city's economic backbone. This became more difficult, however, once large casinos began invading both white and black suburbs. In 1955, Will Max Schwartz opened the Moulin Rouge Casino and Hotel. It was the only integrated resort in Las Vegas.[22] This establishment was officially off limits to members of the Upper Room, but there were exceptions.

Holiness living was the expectation, but allowances were granted in order to make a living. For example, many considered drinking beer a sin, but Francis Harris' husband, Nathan, was allowed to drive a beer truck in the 1950s because "one had to do what one had to do" in order to support one's family. When such exceptions were made, church leaders justified it as a temporary measure until a less controversial job could be secured. However, in Harris' case it turned out to be a long-term position, and he continued to drive a beer truck into the 1970s. Later, he also served as pastor of Gateway to Heaven Church of God in Christ.[23] Nathan Harris' story demonstrates the flexibility within an officially hard-line holiness code.

Much like Pastor Steward's church where theological flexibility countenanced some occupations that would be banned elsewhere and where the role of women in the church was emphasized, the Upper Room also recognized the value of its dedicated female members. The office of "Mother" was the highest formal rank in the church a woman could attain. Women were an important part of church life at the Upper Room Church of God in Christ. While they were not allowed to be ministers or engage in the preaching ministry, they were an important part of the life and ministry of the congregation. There was but one official church mother in the congregation. She was appointed by the pastor and selected on the basis of her life experience and spiritual maturity. The Scriptural foundation for the office was the New Testament epistle to Titus. The first verses of the second chapter dealt with the leadership role of women in the church.

"But as for you, speak the things which are proper for sound doctrine . . . the older women likewise, that they be reverent in behavior, not slanderous, not given to much wine, teaching of good things—that

22. Moehring, *Resort City in the Sunbelt*, 183.
23. Francis Harris. Interview by author, August and September 2000.

they admonish the young women to love their husbands, to love their children, to be discreet, chaste, homemakers, good, obedient to their own husbands, that the word of God may not be blasphemed" (Titus 2:3–5).

One of the roles of the church mother was to be available to offer counsel to the pastor. She also assumed the responsibility of instructing young women in matters of appropriate personal conduct, mothering, and child rearing. The church mother was available to serve as a guidance counselor. Both men and women would go to the mother and seek her help in working through personal problems. There was also an assistant church mother and a mother in training as apprentices being groomed to one day assume the mantel of church mother. On communion Sunday, water baptism Sunday, and on special women's days, the church mother, along with the other women would dress in white and were assigned special seating during worship services. They wore white to set themselves apart and also to symbolize purity and solidarity. In many ways, women and especially the church mother set the spiritual and moral standard for the congregation.[24]

The office of missionary was another important role designated for women. Missionaries in the Church of God in Christ were not Christian ambassadors to some distant land, but lay evangelists who sought to spread the gospel among those in the local community. The church's missionaries often publicly addressed the congregation and also led the charge in seeking new converts to the faith. While the office of pastor was restricted to men, women were an integral part of the congregation's spiritual life.[25] Two tiers of authority existed in the church. Men were the official leaders following the biblical pattern of male leadership in the church. However, on a practical level, women were the church's mainstay. This was not by biblical design, but of practical necessity since so many men did not want to get too involved. There was a frustration among women that more men did not step up and assume roles of meaningful leadership.[26]

It can be argued that the African-American religious community was maternal in many respects. There certainly was a maternal dimension to the Pentecostal practice of faith. It was the church women who were dedicated to the ministry of prayer. They were also in charge of attending

24. Louise Miller. Interview by author, September 2000.

25. Francis Harris. Interview by author, August and September 2000.

26. Ethel Cox. Interview by author, October 2000.

to the practical needs of church members or outsiders in need of food, clothing, or financial assistance. They also assumed the responsibility of "training the younger women in godliness." The idea of a woman's prominence in promoting domesticity extended to women on the Westside, and it was the ministry of the church mothers to instill proper values and behavior patterns into the hearts of the church's younger women.[27]

There was an interesting connection between church and family structure within the local Church of God in Christ. The following account typifies a common perception among many of the Pentecostal women interviewed. The names and details were altered to protect the anonymity of the family involved. Betty Martin moved to Las Vegas in the mid-1950s. She came from a small town in the South and found employment as a maid in one of the hotels. Soon after arriving in Las Vegas, she joined the Upper Room Church of God in Christ. A few years later, Betty met Walter who was in town visiting a family member while recovering from a painful divorce. Walter decided to stay after he found a job, first as a porter and later as a worker at Basic Magnesium. A relationship developed, they fell in love, and were married within a year. Betty's church involvement remained an essential part of her life, but Walter was more of a nominal church member. The two of them were married for many years until Walter's death. Theirs was a stable marriage but one that left Betty frustrated in some respects. She regretted the fact her husband never really took the spiritual lead in their home. The responsibility to maintain the family's spiritual life rested with her, and this was not a role she preferred to take. Mrs. Martin believed in the biblical teaching that husbands are to be the head of the wife and family. However, she felt she had to take the initiative in the absence of her husband's willingness to do so.[28]

Mrs. Martin recalled most families being intact nuclear families into the early 1960s. In recent years, however, the frequency of divorce increased among members of the congregation. Often, it was the wife who initiated the separation. One longtime church member, Mother Ware, speculated economic empowerment motivated some women to

27. Verna Ware. Interview by author, July 2000. Mother Ware was the church mother of Pentecostal Temple Church of God in Christ from 1970–90. She was appointed state church mother in 1994.

28. Betty Martin. Interview by author, October 2000. Fictitious name used by the interviewee at her request since she was still a prominent member of Westside Church and the community.

seek divorce. No longer were they in economic dependency, and so they "just didn't have to take it anymore."[29] Mrs. Martin believed the church bore some responsibility for deteriorating marriages. She felt the church, through the Mother's ministry, did a good job teaching young women how to be good Christian wives and how to relate to their husbands and families. However, there was no such instruction for young men. Betty maintained there should have been a similar program to train men how to be good husbands and spiritual leaders in the home and church especially in a casino city like Las Vegas.

Pentecostals considered members of denominational churches to be worldly Christians at best, and some black Pentecostals questioned whether or not they were genuine "born again" Christians. At least as far as spiritual matters were concerned, Westside Pentecostals were separatists believing themselves to be the real Christians. However, on another level there was a broad sense of community linking together African-Americans across religious lines. On social issues and matters pertaining to civil rights, the entire black citizenry of West Las Vegas stood in solidarity. There were cordial relations between the pastors regardless of church affiliation. Bishop Cox rapidly emerged as a community leader who was admired and respected by other pastors, the general population of that part of town, and the black community at large.

Pastors encouraged church members to be actively involved in matters pertaining to the betterment of their community. Bishop Cox's views regarding social action greatly influenced most of the members of Cox's Upper Room, since many were uneducated and not familiar with the political and social issues. While church members were free to vote their conscience in an election, Cox's congregation expected their pastor to instruct them on how they should vote. The people viewed the pastor as an authority figure. He researched the candidates and provided voting guidance.[30] Bishop Cox was concerned about discrimination and sought to correct injustice through the ballot box and education. He encouraged blacks to seek advancement through education, and was even a

---

29. Verna Ware. Interview by author, July 2000.

30. Group Discussion. Interview by author, August 2000. This discussion group consisted of five women who have been longtime members of the local church of God in Christ. Their names are Georgette Franklin, Francis Harris, Ethel Cox, Louise Miller, and Alberta Davis.

member of the Clark County School District Committee of One Hundred on Integration.[31]

In 1960, the civil rights movement in Las Vegas intensified. That year the local chapter of the NAACP, led by local dentist Dr. James McMillan, organized a march of protest to be held on the Las Vegas Strip. The protest was intended to gain the right for African-Americans to work in all jobs in the casinos and hotels as well as the right to be served at all public establishments. Bishop Cox allowed the marchers to meet at the Upper Room to commence the march. As it turned out, it was cancelled when the hotel owners backed down, agreed to demands, and changed the local segregation practices. Bishop Cox was not outspoken in rhetoric about social activism, but indeed he was an integral part of the effort to abolish local segregation laws. It is doubtful that the existing laws would have been overturned if it had not been for the support of the black churches on the Westside. Cox was clearly one of the most important religious leaders of the black community.

Nevada's Civil Rights Act of 1965 marked another watershed for black Las Vegans. From that year on, African-Americans could legally work in all phases of the hotel, restaurant, and gambling industries. In the 1970s and 1980s, new employment opportunities for black men and women in the casino industry tested the holiness codes of church members from Pentecostal congregations. Before this date, Pentecostal prohibitions about working in questionable places of employment were a moot point because segregation laws kept many blacks from even applying for such jobs.

Many within the Church of God in Christ found the new employment opportunities too good to resist. Over time, the church softened its stance concerning accepted employment for members in good standing. One prominent Church of God minister recollected that the Las Vegas branch of the denomination came to be regarded as too liberal by churches from other parts of the country.[32] Even though there were clear teachings regarding an appropriate Christian lifestyle, standards and expectations were sensitive to the local culture. If church doctrine needed

31. *Fiftieth Jubilee 1941–1991*, 9.

32. Carruth Hall. Interview by author, February 2000. Bishop Hall has been active in the Church of God in Christ since the early 1950s. He has served as pastor of Greater Saint Paul Church of God in Christ since 1964 and has been bishop over the State of Nevada since 1993.

to be recast in order to accommodate the local setting, so be it. Bishop Cox believed education was the key to social and economic advancement. He had a particular interest in educating potential religious leaders. The establishment of Cox Theological Seminary (later renamed the C. H. Mason Theological Seminary) demonstrated the bishop's commitment to education. The seminary was a training center for educating aspiring pastors in the Church of God in Christ. As the denomination grew in the desert valley, most of the local Church of God in Christ leaders were trained at this local institution.[33]

Bishop Cox had a vision that spread beyond his own congregation. It was his dream to establish other Church of God in Christ congregations across the state. Under his sponsorship, Cox oversaw the establishment of two churches in Reno and one in Hawthorne, Nevada. He could rely on a number of pastors among the membership of Upper Room Church of God in Christ and drew upon this resource to supply pastors for the new churches he sponsored. At the time of his death in 1969, there were eighteen Church of God in Christ congregations in Nevada, plus two in California.[34]

Cox encouraged congregants of Upper Room to organize and establish new churches in their neighborhoods. The plan was to form new congregations in local residential neighborhoods of the black community. A small group of parishioners from a residential area would approach Pastor Cox and he would give his blessing, sometimes with limited financial support, to aid their creation of another local Church of God in Christ.[35] The emphasis on starting new churches and seeding them with members of the mother church did not hurt the Upper Room Church of God in Christ. Upper Room grew to include more than one thousand members in the late 1960s while, at the same time, lending people and support to the creation of eighteen new congregations.[36]

Bishop Cox's era ended with his death after a six-month battle with cancer. A wake was held the night before the funeral at the Upper Room Church of God in Christ. Hundreds of mourners came to pay respects to the Westside's "Mr. Pentecost." The next day a large funeral

33. Ibid.

34. *Fiftieth Jubilee 1941–1991*, 9.

35. Carruth Hall. Interview by author, February 2000.

36. Obsequies. Clyde Carson Cox memorial service, February 7, 1969.

service, attended by several hundred people, was held at the South Hall of the Convention Center. A number of prominent politicians, including former Governor Grant Sawyer, Lieutenant Governor Ed Fike, and Mayor Gragson attended the funeral.[37] There were also pastors of other Westside churches and denominational leaders from the Church of God in Christ, who came from across the nation came to pay tribute to the man who meant so much to the growth of Pentecostalism in Nevada. Conspicuously absent from the list of those in attendance were pastors of the local white Pentecostal churches.[38] Their absence underscored the separation between white and black Pentecostal churches. It is doubtful that many white Pentecostals even knew who Bishop Cox was. Among Bishop Cox's many accomplishments was the establishment of churches in the state of Nevada, appointment as secretary of the Judiciary Board of the International Church of God in Christ, and personal guide to Bishop C. H. Mason, senior bishop of the Church of God in Christ. Cox also served as a member of the Las Vegas City Planning Commission, the Juvenile Justice Commission, and the Clark County School District Committee of One Hundred on Integration.[39]

Reverend Earnest Napoleon Webb succeeded Cox. Webb was an understudy of Cox and was chosen by him to be his eventual successor. His personality and style was different from Cox in that he was more businesslike and less approachable than Cox. Webb was more of an organizer, administrator, and builder. His wife, Mattie Belle, was a homemaker who supported her husband's ministry away from the spotlight. Webb lacked the advantage of a formal education but was an avid reader and a self-educated man. As a preacher, he, too, was "jubilistic" in style.

Webb continued the Cox tradition of being a respected community leader. For a number of years he served on the board of directors of Valley Hospital. He was an ambitious builder. Under his leadership, the Upper Room Church of God in Christ was radically remodeled and enlarged. A fire started by an arsonist provided the occasion for the enlargement. In 1976 this arsonist, for motives never revealed, set fire to several churches on the Westside, but committed suicide before going to trial. The local newspaper reported, "Cox Upper Room Church . . . was totally

37. Louise Miller. Interview by author, September 2000.

38. Obsequies. Clyde Carson Cox memorial service, February 7, 1969.

39. Ibid.

destroyed."[40] Under Webb's leadership the church was rebuilt, enlarged, and re-named Pentecostal Temple.

The Church of God in Christ was the dominant black Pentecostal denomination in Las Vegas, but it was not the only one. According to incomplete Sunday School records, Christ Holy Sanctified Church organized locally in 1952 by a woman, Lola Hayes, who also served as pastor.[41] The doctrinal beliefs that distinguished Christ Holy Sanctified Church from the Church of God in Christ were the practice of ritual foot washing, pacifism, and the ordination of women.[42]

The Church of God in Christ did not ordain women into the pulpit ministry, yet Hayes felt the call and gained her ministerial credentials through the Christ Holy Sanctified Church. Before starting the new church she was a member of Second Baptist, but after receiving the Pentecostal experience of "speaking in tongues," she had a vision that prompted her to pioneer a new church. Missionaries representing the Christ Holy Sanctified denomination came to Las Vegas and Hayes met with them. She decided to affiliate with the small Pentecostal denomination and began holding church services in her home at 316 West Madison Avenue.[43]

Reverend Hayes was a strong-willed woman who opposed the trend toward a male-dominated clergy. She pastored a church even though it was not a broadly accepted thing for a woman to do. Earlier in her life she had been married, but it ended in divorce. Hayes never remarried but dedicated the rest of her life to the ministry. She was an evangelist at heart, serving as pastor of Christ Holy Sanctified from 1952 through 1956. Hayes returned to the church in 1957 and stepped down as pastor in 1965. Throughout her ministry career she also traveled to northern Nevada, California, and southern states ministering as an evangelist.[44]

Hayes was very strict in her understanding of the Christian life. She did not believe a Christian woman should wear any make-up and that

40. "Cox Church Ravaged by Big Blaze," September 29, 1976.

41. Sunday School records. Bishop Herman Ishmael of Christ Holy Sanctified Church allowed the viewing of Sunday School records which dated the beginning of the church's history as 1952.

42. King, *Discipline of Christ Holy Sanctified Church of America*, 11, 22.

43. Hermann Ishmael. Interview by author, December 2001. Bishop Ishmael has been a member of Christ Holy Sanctified Church since 1952. He served as pastor from 1976–2000.

44. Ibid.

they must always wear long sleeves to cover their arms. In her view it was inappropriate for church members to attend sporting events, the theater, dance or gamble. Under Reverend Hayes' ministry, the Pentecostal code was interpreted so narrowly that her ministry was limited in scope. Her congregation did not grow as large as did the Church of God in Christ. At its peak, it never had more than fifty members.[45] The Church of God in Christ adapted itself to the local environment while Christ Holy Sanctified held the line on the traditional holiness codes. Hayes was not as multi-dimensional in her understanding of the Gospel as was Bishop Cox. She never was involved in community activism nor did she participate in the civil rights movement. Her understanding of the gospel was that it applied to matters of the heart and spirit, not to political or community matters.

During the 1970s, the black subculture that had been historically confined to the Westside was breaking up. High-paying jobs in Las Vegas provided a higher standard of living for many African-Americans. In 1971, there was a federal consent decree mandating the hotels and casinos to hire black men for all jobs for which they were professionally qualified. Black women received the same right in 1981. Also in 1971, Governor Mike O'Callaghan signed an open housing law that ended residential segregation. Like other upwardly mobile Americans, many blacks sought better housing and moved into the new housing tracks springing up across the valley. Churches retained their status as the glue of the black community, but they were becoming more and more like drive-in religious centers. They were scattered around the Westside, but by the 1980s, most members lived in the suburbs.[46] Their only connection with the Westside was the churches to which they commuted on Sundays. As the flock scattered, it was less important for the church doors be opened every night of the week. There were now other things to do besides attend church. It took more of an effort to go to church than it did when the church was part of the neighborhood. Some of the changes were also evident in the congregation's worship services. Services were still quite long, but Sunday worship was no longer an all-day affair.[47]

There was a higher economic standard of living for many African-Americans due to their educational achievements and open job market. A

45. Ibid.

46. Carruth Hall. Interview by author, February 2000.

47. Ethel Cox. Interview by author, October 2000.

more educated laity also exerted an impact on voting patterns of behavior within local congregations. It became less important for the pastor to endorse a political candidate for the congregation. Church members now considered themselves to be better informed and tended to make those decisions independent of pastoral advice.

The same process of cultural assimilation that characterized other denominations was at work in the Church of God in Christ. This phenomenon was not unique to local black Pentecostals. It was exemplified by church music. Black gospel music has long been popular in all sectors of American culture. In 1963 a former assistant pastor under Bishop Cox, Elder Carruth Hall, left the congregation of Upper Room to establish a new church on North G Street. He began with a congregation of just five people. As the church grew, it developed a personality and emphasis all its own. The Halls were a musical family, and by the 1970s their church had an outstanding music ministry. In 1973, their choir was asked to back up Paul Anka who was performing at the Riviera Hotel. That same year, Natalie Cole asked the choir to back her up at the MGM Grand Hotel. The relationship was a good one, and they performed together through the 1990s. It is doubtful the Church of God in Christ in earlier years would have sanctioned such performances. As the congregation became more of a mainstream, middle-class group, members reinterpreted their standards to better fit a new cultural reality. They put a theological spin on their foray into the entertainment industry. Pastor Hall reasoned that the choir's presence on stage presented a new opportunity to bring the gospel to people who would never enter the church.[48]

The color line remained a point of division among Pentecostals in Las Vegas. There was not much interaction between black and white churches. In the early years there had been integrated congregations at Zion Rest Mission, the Westside Church, and the Foursquare Church, but, as the churches developed, they became quite segregated and independent of one another. The one exception to this was the Billy Graham crusades of 1978 and 1980. African-American Pentecostals were active participants in those two events.[49] Their racial separatism did not seem to be a matter of great concern, as both blacks and whites were quite content to practice their faith separately.

48. Carruth Hall. Interview by author, February 2000.
49. Ibid.

The revival on the Las Vegas Strip, which occurred during the middle 1970s and extended into the 1980s, did not infiltrate the black Pentecostal community. These Pentecostals formed a more self-contained community and operated as a sub-culture unto themselves. Their churches did not experience the same influx of employees from the Strip that white Pentecostal/Evangelical churches did.[50]

The African-American Pentecostals of Las Vegas were more politically involved than their white counterparts. Bishop Cox was actively engaged with local community issues. He served on a number of community boards and agencies and was a participant in the local civil rights movement. The black Pentecostal church perpetuated the tradition of the church being a center of community life. This was a legacy that extended back to the era of slavery when the church was the only forum where slaves could interact and discuss their real life grievances.[51] In contrast, white Pentecostals remained disconnected from general community issues with the exception of the right to life issue in the 1980s.

The historiographic literature emphasizes this point. In his classic study of religious patterns in America, H. Richard Niebuhr in *Christ and Culture* contended that disenfranchised groups of people tended to organize separatist communities of faith that defined them apart from the cultural mainstream. However, assimilation inevitably occurred as succeeding generations of Christians bettered themselves educationally and economically.[52] They entered into society's mainstream and formed middle class churches. This pattern of upward mobility and cultural assimilation was evident in the development of black Pentecostalism in Las Vegas. Robert Mapes Anderson, in *Vision of the Disinherited*, made a similar point. Anderson contended that strict holiness codes emphasizing personal piety, evangelistic zeal, apocalyptic eschatology, and cultural separatism were characteristics of marginalized groups of people.[53] Those without a reasonable hope in the temporal world tended to separate themselves from the mainstream and "super naturalize" the object of

50. Carruth Hall. Interview by author, February 2000.

51. Genovese, *Roll Jordon Roll*, 236.

52. Niebuhr, *The Social Sources of Denominationalism*, 26–53. This classic study by Niebuhr identified the characteristics and movement of Christians from the disinherited class into the economic and social mainstream.

53. Anderson, *Vision of the Disinherited*, 195–222.

their hope. Westside black Pentecostals fit the mold as described both by Niebuhr and Anderson.

The influx of African-Americans into Las Vegas' Westside community consisted largely of disenfranchised blacks coming west in the hope they could escape the grinding poverty they had previously experienced. Their Pentecostal faith provided a context in which they could disavow participation in the mainstream culture that had rejected them. The church became their community, and their hope focused on the apocalyptic in-breaking of the kingdom of God. As their faith took root, and they applied biblical principles of honesty and the Protestant work ethic, they began to move up the economic ladder. Many became part of an emerging black middle-class. In time, this caused them to rethink their traditional concept of separation from the world. At least in the work place, separation became more of a spiritual or inward reality and had less to do with one's outward actions.

6

Revival on the Las Vegas Strip

THE REVIVAL ON THE Strip marked a breakthrough in the effective marketing of the Pentecostal message to relate to the local culture. During the 1970s and 1980s, Pentecostals learned how to "play Vegas." Their pragmatism triumphed as they reformatted old holiness codes to include converts from various expressions of the local "sin" industry. However, there was a price that was paid. When the line between spirit and flesh was blurred there was sometimes a trade off. The Spirit did transform many broken lives, but sometimes the flesh corrupted spiritual people. Be that as it may, this period marked the emergence of Pentecostal Christianity as a major player within the greater Las Vegas religious community.

Nevada has always been considered a renegade state, both culturally and religiously: a remnant of the frontier West. A 1974 study ranked Nevada as forty-sixth among the fifty states in religious adherence.[1] A 1982 survey of religion in America identified Nevada as the least religious state in the union.[2] However, a Las Vegas revival occurred during the 1970s that helped contribute to the emergence of a strong Pentecostal community of faith. Local churches, backstage Bible studies, KILA radio, and the Billy Graham Crusades were all components of a spiritual awakening. This spiritual renaissance resulted in a visible sub-culture, which espoused a conservative theology and traditional morality.

What is interesting for the purpose of this inquiry is the fact that Las Vegas charismatics, during the time period being considered, were

1. Associated Press. "Utah Most Religious State," *Las Vegas Review Journal*, July 27, 1974.

2. Associated Press. "Nevada Trails States in Religious Adherence," *Las Vegas Review Journal*, October 2, 1982.

not clones of those in other parts of the nation. Charismatics call for separatism from the world. The theological nomenclature for this tenet of faith is "holiness living." Consumption of alcoholic beverages, usage of tobacco, questionable entertainment, gambling, and often times working on Sunday were ingredients of a lifestyle inconsistent with their definition of acceptable Christian living. What made some Las Vegas Pentecostals of the 1970s and 1980s interesting was how they differed so dramatically from their counterparts elsewhere in America.

In this chapter the term "charismatic" and "evangelical" will be frequently employed because a revival that occurred in Las Vegas during the 1970s and 1980s embraced more than just classical Pentecostals. By the 1970s, Pentecostal elements of spirituality had infiltrated into many mainstream Christian churches and religious organizations. Many charismatic Christians during the decades of the 1980s and 1990s were at once actively involved in Pentecostal or evangelical churches and, at the same time, employed in professions usually considered taboo for individuals of such religious persuasion. Indeed, many active charismatics were also engaged in a revival centering among show people on the Las Vegas Strip. There is evidence to support their claim. Pentecostal/charismatic churches, as well as home Bible studies, experienced unusual growth that included the conversion of entertainers. Those involved in the revival were a Bible-centered people and members of local churches that prohibited consumption of alcohol, dancing, erotic entertainment, gambling, and a host of other perceived vices. Yet a surprising number of converts continued to be involved in both the church and the city's entertainment industry.

The strength of Pentecostalism in Las Vegas is evidenced by several factors. Since the 1930s, there have been a growing number of Pentecostal churches. KILA Christian radio was founded in July 1972, and since the 1970s has been one of the most popular radio stations in the city.[3] KILA was not officially a Pentecostal radio station, but it drew a large listening audience from among Pentecostals and at least one Pentecostal church, Trinity Temple, financially supported this ministry.

Las Vegas was certainly not the only place where this brand of faith thrived. Various surveys concluded that 34 percent of the American public claimed a born-again religious experience. That percentage has held

3. Jack French. Interview by author, March 1992. Mr. French is owner and manager of KILA radio station established in Las Vegas in 1972.

steady since the early 1980s.[4] Harvey Cox is one among several American religious authorities who believes charismatics are becoming part of the new religious mainstream.[5]

The basis of spiritual or religious authority for Pentecostals is important to understand in order to grasp the distinct character of the Las Vegas brand of charismatic faith. For fundamentalists it is simply a matter of what the Bible literally says. Fundamentalists insist that every word in the Bible must be accepted as literally true, and call this doctrine "verbal inspiration."[6] For instance, a strict fundamentalist will not allow women to serve in the pastoral ministry because a literal reading of St. Paul's letters forbade the practice. The Pentecostal and charismatic also seeks to follow scripture but not with the same literalism as fundamentalists. It is the Bible as illuminated and prioritized by the Holy Spirit that serves as the ultimate authority. For them, there is not an absolute way to interpret Scripture. They count on the "leading of the Holy Spirit" to provide understanding of how the specific teachings of the Bible apply. Theirs is a more pneumatic hermeneutic. They are also more contextual and fluid in their Biblicism.

Charismatics of every stripe interpret themselves as a people of the Book. This presented a special challenge for charismatics who live in the culture and economy of Las Vegas. Pentecostals involved in the gaming and entertainment industry of Las Vegas found themselves caught up in a lifestyle that was incompatible with traditional Pentecostalism.

The period from the early 1970s through the mid-1980s was a particularly interesting and distinctive time for the religious community of Las Vegas. There was a spiritual awakening among many employees in the entertainment industry that brought a new type of believer into the charismatic fold. Exotic dancers (including strippers and show dancers), ice skaters, and showgirls were among the more female converts. There were also some professional gamblers, dealers, and pit bosses who converted. These converts comprised a highly atypical Pentecostal constituency because their professional careers did not conform to either commonly held holiness codes or the practice of separation from the world. Despite their unconventional ways, many eventually gravitated to local churches while

4. Barna, *What Americans Believe*, 179.

5. Cox, *Fire From Heaven*, 15–16.

6. Marsden, *Fundamentalism*, 118–23.

others identified with backstage Bible study groups. It was also during this period that KILA radio was established and became a popular voice of inspiration and spiritual guidance for these converts who worked on the Las Vegas Strip.

During the 1970s and 1980s, Trinity Temple was the largest Protestant congregation in Nevada. It was instrumental in the spread of the charismatic renewal throughout the valley and played a vital role in the development of the broader local evangelical community. Throughout Trinity's early history, it remained a strict traditional holiness church (see chapter 4). The church denied membership to individuals employed at the casinos.[7] One former board member recalls a conversation in the 1960s between the pastor and a guest musician scheduled to sing in the Sunday evening service. After the morning service, the pastor took the visiting musician to lunch at a local resort. The guest naively dropped a nickel into a slot machine whereupon the pastor informed him that if he pulled the lever he would not be allowed to sing in church that night.[8]

Things changed dramatically beginning in 1971 when the church called Bill Sharp to fill the pulpit.[9] The Sharp ministry brought a high public profile to the Temple. Sharp produced a film for circulation among other churches entitled "Las Vegas, My Kind of Town." He claimed that a number of popular entertainers were interested in his ministry. He personally baptized pop country singer Judy Lynn, and a well-known local entertainer, Chico Holiday, converted and later joined the pastoral staff of Trinity Temple.[10] The years of Pastor Sharp's ministry were at once engaging, controversial, and volatile. He brought a flash and style that was foreign to the holiness-minded Pentecostal church. His dashing appearance captured the imagination of his followers, and his spellbinding oratory convinced many to respond to his invitation to accept Christ as Savior. He was infatuated with the glitter of Vegas and called himself the "Chaplain of the Strip."[11] Sharp published a monthly

7. Ellenore Nighswonger. Interview by author, October 1992. Mrs. Nighswonger became a member of Trinity in 1931. She is the daughter of Emma Jacobson.

8. Eldron Grauberger. Interviews by author September and October 1994. Personal diary, January 1974. Mr. Grauberger served as a board member of Trinity during Bill Sharp's pastorate.

9. New Dimension Magazine.

10. Tell: Trinity's Envoy of Light and Life.

11. Vita Souza. Interview by author, September 1992. Mrs. Souza was active at Trinity since the early 1950s. She was Women's Ministries director during the 1960s.

magazine highlighting his ministry in the city. He was a master promoter who knew how to get the public's attention.[12] A board member during the Sharp years expressed his initial support for Sharp's unconventional ministry by stating, "I was suspicious of his tactics, but he was filling the church and people were getting saved."[13]

But not everyone got caught up in the excitement. As noted earlier, controversy began to plague Pastor Sharp's tenure at Trinity Temple. Some congregants raised questions concerning the pastor's personal life, and members of the official board saw irregularities in the handling of church finances. There were accusations of womanizing and charges he had funneled church money into his own personal ministry called New Dimensions.[14] Board member Eldon Grauberger produced copies of altered checks to support the accusations, and the church board accused Sharp of embezzling thousands of dollars. Ultimately, Pastor Sharp paid back $5,000 but denied he had taken more.[15]

Matters came to a head in 1974 when the official church board asked Sharp to leave Trinity Temple. It was not an amiable separation. He left under a cloud of controversy that split the church. His breakaway congregation initially met at the Landmark Hotel. Sharp's goal was to purchase the Landmark Hotel and turn it into a Christian resort and religious center.[16] Sharp declared that he was not dismissed from the Assemblies of God as a credentialed minister, but he voluntarily gave up his papers in order to stay in Las Vegas and begin another Pentecostal ministry. A local newspaper contradicted Sharp's statement.[17] When directly asked if there was any basis to the charges of financial mismanagement and philandering, Sharp simply replied that no allegation against him was ever proven.[18]

12. *Tell: Trinity's Envoy of Light and Life.*

13. Eldon Grauberger. Interview by author September and October 1994. Personal diary, January 1974. Mr. Grauberger served as a board member of Trinity during Bill Sharp's pastorate.

14. Ibid.

15. Minutes. Trinity Temple official board minutes from 1974.

16. Greg Massanari. Interview by author, October 1994. Rev. Massanari pastored another charismatic church in Las Vegas (Christian Life Community) during the 1980s. He was also a close personal acquaintance with several in leadership at Calvary Chapel/Dove Ministries.

17. Fredrick, "Fast Living Pastor Oversees Bankrupt Church."

18. Bill Sharp. Interview by author, January 2002. Rev. Sharp was pastor of Trinity Temple.

After leaving the Landmark Hotel, Sharp began to conduct Sunday afternoon services at the Circus Circus Hotel. The ministry there grew into the hundreds. After a few months at the resort, Sharp relocated his fledgling ministry to the Showboat Hotel. However, according to him, his group was soon asked to leave the Showboat because his followers passed out religious tracts on the casino floor. Sharp and his band of followers relocated once again to the Wild World of Burlesque, located on the Strip.[19]

Within a year of leaving Trinity, Sharp negotiated a deal to purchase the Centerama Theater on Paradise Road. For a time, the new work flourished and became a prominent place of worship during the years of the revival on the Strip. Sharp's ability to attract the interest of celebrities continued. On a number of occasions Robert Goulet gave Christian performances at Centerama and Pat Boone appeared on the platform as a guest singer. Other entertainers who visited the church included Wayne Newton, Lola Folana, Johnny Mathis, and Clint Eastwood. Liberace even donated a white grand piano to the church. Sharp also became active in Las Vegas' lucrative wedding industry, working as a supply minister for various Strip wedding chapels. He officiated at weddings three times on the Merv Griffin television show.[20]

Sharp's genius for promotion continued during his tenure at Centerama. He publicized his ministry nationally and attracted some leading televangelists. He appeared with Pat Robertson on the 700 Club, and Jim and Tammy Bakker's PTL program once featured Centerama as the national "church of the month." He caught the attention of nationally known evangelist Katheryn Kuhlman, and she came to the Convention Center for a healing service.[21]

By 1978, Centerama was in financial trouble and filed for chapter 11 bankruptcy. Sharp's high profile style of ministry could not be sustained through the free-will offerings of the congregation. There was also a storm of controversy swirling around the Sharps' personal lives. They were accused of lavish living while the church was headed for bankruptcy. They each drove Lincoln Continentals, took vacations in Hawaii, and wore expensive clothes and lots of expensive jewelry. He even received an honorary doctor of divinity degree from Union University Graduate

19. Ibid.
20. Ibid.
21. Ibid.

School after sending them a financial donation. The legitimacy of this degree was questionable because it came from a school that offered a degree in oriental medicine but had no classes in religious studies.[22] In addition, accusations persisted concerning Bill Sharp's personal life. In the end, the weight of debt and controversy proved too great a burden and the church closed its doors. Centerama was an independent legal corporation and had no denominational backing to help it through the financial crisis. In Bankruptcy Court the judge praised Sharp for being a gifted promoter but offered this counterpoint, "You're not a good businessman."[23]

In the end, Sharp's attempt to reconcile the Strip and the church foundered because of his own ethical and moral weaknesses. However, to his credit and despite personal shortcomings, Sharp knew how to draw a crowd and recognized the gospel was fluid enough to be creatively adapted. The local Pentecostals were traditionally rock-ribbed separatists, but Sharp managed to redefine the relationship between the entertainment industry and the religious community. A new breed of parishioner began attending churches. Sharp helped open a pathway through which others would pass as the Las Vegas revival continued to grow.

During the period when Sharp was developing Centerama, Trinity Temple regrouped and became a larger and more prominent church than ever. In the late 1970s and 1980s, Trinity claimed several thousand adherents.[24] Trinity conducted two Sunday morning worship services that were both consistently filled. Four hundred to five hundred more people came for the Sunday evening service. The total Sunday attendance averaged nearly 2,000.[25] On Easter Sunday, approximately 5,000 attended, and it required the police to direct traffic and five services to accommodate the crowds.

Trinity was the largest and most influential Protestant church in town and it served as a conduit linking charismatic faith to the Strip. The remembrances of some of the converts make the point. Doyle "Dolly" Brunson, for instance, was a professional gambler who made his living

22. Fredrick, "Fast Living Pastor Oversees Bankrupt Church," *Las Vegas Review Journal*, September 30, 1979.

23. Ibid.

24. Melvin and Norma Steward. Interview by author, October 1994 and January 2002. Rev. Steward pastored Trinity from 1974–84.

25. Hilda Wagenknecht. Interview by author, April 1992. Rev. Wagenknecht was Trinity's record keeper from 1975–98.

as a poker player. His wife began attending Trinity Temple in the early 1970s, but Dolly was not religious and even threatened to divorce his wife if she continued attending church. His attitude towards the Pentecostal faith changed, however, after his daughter died from anorexia. His daughter's demise caused him to re-evaluate his life, which led him to become a born again charismatic Christian.

Brunson realized his gambling was at odds with his religion, but he resisted quitting since it was his business and a significant source of income. Instead of giving it up, Brunson wanted God to bless his gambling and once asked the pastor to attend a poker championship with him and pray that God would help him win. Doyle began to tithe 10 percent on his poker winnings and once gave $50,000 cash to help establish an Assemblies of God church in Pahrump, Nevada. There was never any pressure exerted by the church to quit gambling, but it was something that bothered Brunson.[26]

A man remembered only as Kramer professed a conversion experience in the early 1980s. He became actively involved at Trinity but continued his job as a bartender. This was controversial because Pentecostals strictly opposed the consumption of alcoholic beverages. Kramer understood but believed that the Lord wanted him to continue tending bar because there he could share his faith people who never entered churches. Kramer personally quit drinking, brought a Bible with him to work, and kept it with him at the bar. On several occasions he had opportunity to counsel individuals who were depressed or searching for spiritual solutions. He continued tending bar for a few years until he felt "released." Eventually, Kramer quit bartending and moved to the Midwest where he began a new career.[27]

A number of dancers and showgirls attended Trinity Temple in the late 1970s and early 1980s. One was Dawn Cottingham. She was a topless dancer in some of the hotel lounge acts. She performed at the Marina, Tropicana, Stardust, and MGM hotels. Dawn was involved with drugs, alcohol, sexual promiscuity, and once had an abortion to maintain her figure. Dawn was afraid she might lose her job if it were known she was pregnant. She harbored a deep-seated guilt and experienced a growing emptiness which led her to dabble in meditation and other expressions

26. Melvin and Norma Steward. Interview by author, October 1994 and January 2002. Rev. Steward pastored Trinity from 1974–84.

27. Ibid.

of popular spirituality. Meditation, Eastern religion, and the occult were common forms of spirituality among show people.[28] Dawn was searching for depth and meaning in her life and felt debased by performing topless. In 1977, she produced a new "covered" show called "Viva Las Vegas." A group of dancers were recruited, and they traveled to Acapulco, Mexico, to perform in a hotel there. Dawn met a born-again dancer and converted to evangelical Christianity. The rest of the "Viva Las Vegas" dance team was so impressed with the change in Dawn's life, they also converted. Soon after they contacted some missionaries working in Mexico and were advised to become involved in a Bible-centered church once they returned to Las Vegas.[29]

Trinity Temple was their church of choice. Dawn and her friends liked the energized worship. The congregation clapped their hands to the beat of up-tempo music; they applauded after choir specials and solos, and were animated in their worship and praise. It reminded her of some of the things she liked best about the entertainment industry. Most importantly, Dawn felt "unconditionally loved" and accepted by the people of the church. No one there condemned her or required her to leave her profession.

Condemnation did come but from a surprising source. Criticism came from other, unconverted show people with whom she worked. They were the ones who were judgmental and who stereotyped how Christians should live. There was a consistent undercurrent of criticism and snide remarks made by her fellow workers about a supposed Christian's involvement in topless entertainment.[30] Dawn began to feel convicted because there was a growing conflict between her faith and her profession. Although her career was at its height and there were lucrative offers to continue dancing, Dawn felt something was wrong. She decided to leave show business even though it meant a loss of income. She left dancing to become a cocktail waitress and said she never regretted the decision.[31] A number of other dancers eventually put Trinity to the test by applying for full membership. After much deliberation, the board of directors decided it was not for them to stand in judgment and exclude these Strip workers

---

28. Dawn Cottingham. Interview by author, November 1994. Ms. Cottingham was a dancer who performed with various Las Vegas strip shows in the late 1970s.

29. Ibid.

30. Ibid.

31. Ibid.

from full church membership. If these women professed a faith in Jesus Christ and met the other church requirements, they should be accepted.[32]

Trinity and Centerama were not the only centers of revival. In the late 1960s, Reverend Jim Reid was a Southern Baptist pastor in the suburb of Henderson. His church consisted of only sixteen members, and he had little contact with the Las Vegas Strip. The turning point in Reid's ministry occurred in the 1970s when he followed up on a convert with the unlikely name of Tallulah Bankhead. Miss Bankhead was a stripper, and Reid paid a pastoral visit to her show in order to encourage her in her fledgling faith. He said contact with the entertainer introduced him to a "mission field that was largely untouched." Reverend Reid's ministry took a new direction. He resigned his church and began "hanging around the Strip playing casino games and chess with stars and dealers, musicians and cocktail waitresses."[33] Soon, he proposed a backstage Bible study for employees at the Dunes Hotel.

From April I, 1977, until April 1, 1985, Jim Reid ministered in the hotels and casinos along Las Vegas Boulevard. He was known as the "Strip Chaplain." Reid's unusual ministry gained national acclaim. *The New York Times*,[34] *The Chicago Daily News*,[35] *The Sunday Oklahoman*,[36] *The Richmond-Times Dispatch*,[37] *The Kansas City Star*,[38] *The Atlanta Journal & Constitution*,[39] and *The Wall Street Journal*[40] are some of the newspapers that published articles about Reid's unorthodox ministry during the decade of the 1970s. The *St. Louis Globe Democrat Sunday Magazine*, [41]

32. Melvin and Norma Steward. Interview by author, October 1994 and January 2002.

33. Jim Reid. Interview by author, January 1995. Rev. Reid was the self-designated "Chaplain of the Strip." He held Bible Studies for entertainers.

34. "A Las Vegas Preacher Ministers to Gamblers & Showgirls," (special to *The New York Times*, October 7, 1973).

35. Marshall, "Las Vegas Chaplain Winning the Loser," *Chicago Daily News*, November 8–9, 1975.

36. Brown, "Minister to Las Vegas Sin Row, That's Jim Reid," *Sunday Oklahoman*, Summer 1974.

37. *Richmond-Times Dispatch*. "People in the News," wire dispatch, October 8, 1973.

38. Brown, "Minister to Casino Strip," *Kansas City Star*, September 8, 1974.

39. Murray, "Strip Chaplain," *Atlanta Journal and Constitution*, February 11, 1978.

40. Cooper, "Room Service? Send 3 Bourbon, 2 Scotch—And One Chaplain," *Wall Street Journal*, May 21, 1974.

41. Marshall, "Praising God on the Las Vegas Strip," *St. Louis Globe Democrat Sunday Magazine*, September 21, 1975, 6–7.

The Nevadan, [42] and *Gallery*[43] (a men's adult entertainment magazine), all featured Jim Reid and his ministry on the Las Vegas Strip.

Jim Reid was a former marine and later worked in an auto parts store before entering the ministry.[44] Reid considered himself a liberal, charismatic Pentecostal who held credentials with the staunchly conservative Southern Baptist denomination. He did not believe in the inerrancy of Scripture. Reverend Reid had an emerging but privately held belief in reincarnation, and in universal salvation.[45] Of course, he was careful to not broadcast his controversial points of theology among fundamentalist Southern Baptists.

In 1970, the Southern Baptist Convention appointed Reid as missionary to Las Vegas, where he opened a new church called "Church on the Strip." It was affiliated with the Southern Baptist Convention and originally met at Duffey's Tavern across the street from Vegas World on the Strip. The Southern Baptists provided the bulk of the funding for the evangelistic endeavor.[46] Reid began Bible studies backstage at most of the major hotels. At the height of the ministry in the mid-1970s, he conducted at least one Bible study every week night and five services on Sunday. The hotel owners did not know all this was occurring on their property, but those working in the shows knew of his ministry. In 1974 alone, Reid baptized 104 new converts. He held a Christmas Eve service at the Dunes Hotel in 1974, and over 1,000 people attended. Reid reported that his Sunday services and backstage Bible studies had "hundreds in attendance every week."[47]

Reid did not preach a message of condemnation. Instead, he emphasized the love, acceptance, and forgiveness found in Jesus Christ. He let the Holy Spirit do the convicting and commented, "It's up to them whether they change their lifestyles or occupations. Christ sets you free."[48] In the course of time, most of the converts forsook questionable employments and lifestyles, but their decisions were based on their own choices and

42. Answer Man on KILA Christian radio in Las Vegas from 1971–78.

43. Black, "The Strip Minister," *Gallery*, June 1976, 85.

44. Ibid.

45. Jim Reid. Interview by author, January 1995. Rev. Reid was the self-designated Chaplain of the Strip. He held Bible studies for entertainers.

46. Ibid.

47. Ibid.

48. Chandler, "Preacher Ministers to Vegas Strip," *Los Angeles Times*, March 24, 1974.

not pressure exerted by the Church on the Strip.[49] Reid had to contend with a plethora of occult activity. "I've fought the Devil. Oh yes. Right here in Las Vegas . . . I've fought demons," he claimed Reid in an interview with *Gallery* magazine.[50] The local entertainment culture was awash with interest in Eastern philosophy, transcendental meditation, Satanism, and other expressions of the occult. Reid believed it significant enough to pursue doctoral studies at San Francisco Theological Seminary and wrote a dissertation on the occult. Reid performed a number of exorcisms during this time.[51]

At the height of his popularity in 1974, Reid was invited to be the featured speaker at the Southern Baptist Women's Ministry Union, a meeting that drew over 7,000 people. They gathered to hear how God transformed Las Vegas sinners and turned them into pious Baptists. But, the Baptist women were horrified to hear that the liberal charismatic missionary did not demand his converts be conformed to conventional Christian lifestyles. Needless to say, he was never invited back.[52] Reid's maverick reputation ultimately caught up with him. He eventually fell into disfavor with denominational leaders and was passed over for other assignments.

Nevertheless, Reid continued to minister as the Strip Chaplain. His work later included both a television and radio program in addition to Bible studies. He also wrote a book chronicling his ministry in Las Vegas entitled *Praising God on the Las Vegas Strip*.[53] In 1985, citing exhaustion, Reid retired from the ministry. The Strip Chaplain was yet another example of charismatic vitality during the decades of the 1970s and 1980s. And there were others. Ken and Virginia Jones moved to Las Vegas in 1971. Ken was a stagehand and lights engineer and Gini was a dancer. Gini had been in show business since age thirteen, so it was natural to come to Las Vegas and seek work on the Strip. She was hired to skate in "Nudes on Ice" at the Hacienda Hotel. About the same time, Ken and Gini began reading the Bible together. In the course of time, they met Jim Reid and began attending one of his Bible studies. The weekly gathering Ken

---

49. Ibid.
50. Black, "The Strip Minister," *Gallery*, June 1976, 85.
51. Jim Reid. Interview by author, January 1995.
52. Ibid.
53. Reid, *Praising God on the Las Vegas Strip*.

and Gini attended was at the Desert Inn Hotel. They later quit attending Reid's Bible studies, because they felt he did not believe in a literal interpretation of all Scripture. They were particularly disturbed because Reid did not subscribe to a literal interpretation of the biblical account of the flood.[54] But theirs was a selective literalism. On one hand, Gini was not initially convicted over her part in erotic ice dancing even though the Bible directly requires proper dress and modesty. On the other hand, the couple was disturbed because Reverend Reid questioned the historical accuracy of a biblical account.[55]

Gini professed a conversion experience at the Episcopal Church in Henderson. A charismatic priest named Father George was the rector there. At the conclusion of a Sunday morning service, Gini responded to an invitation to come forward for prayer. She began to weep and recalled an overwhelming sensation that "Jesus is real." This was the spiritual turning point in her personal life, but it did not immediately change her professional life. Gini became a fervent charismatic and was instrumental in the conversion of eight other dancers in the show. The show came to be nicknamed "Christ on Ice." Gini continued dancing and skating until 1975.[56] Gini left show business after a battle with her conscience. She reluctantly agreed to dance topless in "Minsky's Burlesque" at the Aladdin Hotel but felt guilty about it. Being the lead dancer did not ease the conviction she was doing something wrong. Gini talked the matter over with her husband, they agreed she should quit, and she did so immediately, leaving show business for good. Gini came to believe the performers were controlled by the shows' producers and choreographers who demanded acquiescence without regard for the feelings, values, or morals of the dancers and showgirls. Gini felt compromised and her freedom disrespected. The decision to change careers brought a sense of personal liberation. A sense of dignity was restored and Gini was finally master of her own destiny.[57]

Open minded pastors were crucial to the conversion and recruitment of people like Gini, and Reverend Bob DeVilbiss was another clergyman who made this kind of contribution to Las Vegas Pentecostalism.

---

54. Ken and Jenny Jones. Interview by author, October 1994. Mrs. Jones was a dancer on the Las Vegas Strip during the 1970s.

55. Ibid.

56. Ibid.

57. Ibid.

In the spring of 1971, he and his family came to Las Vegas. DeVilbiss received his theological training at the staunchly conservative Bob Jones University. This was one of the strictest fundamentalist training centers in the United States. At Bob Jones, social contact between the sexes was carefully controlled. No student was allowed to date without being accompanied by a chaperone. It was an unlikely environment to prepare one for ministry in Sin City. After graduation from Bob Jones, DeVilbiss was ordained in the Swedish Baptist denomination, and during the next several years, pastored small congregations in Missouri, Arkansas, and Pennsylvania. DeVilbiss gradually moved away from dogmatic fundamentalism and joined the charismatic movement. He moved to Las Vegas at the invitation of Jack French. Together, they planned to begin a religiously-oriented radio station to be named KILA. DeVilbiss came to host a program called "The Bible Answer Man". It was a call-in show broadcast nightly from 10:00 p.m. until 11:30 p.m.[58]

The Bible Answer Man soon became popular, and many Strip entertainers listened to the program while backstage. Some of them encouraged DeVilbiss to schedule Bible studies that catered to the work schedules of show people. Eventually, there were five organized weekly Bible studies that drew over two hundred people. The success of the Bible studies inspired DeVilbiss to establish a new church called the People's Church. The congregation he pastored grew to include about two hundred and fifty parishioners, many of whom were entertainers.[59]

In 1976, Janie Tacker, an attractive ice-skater, was hired to appear in the Hacienda Hotel's show "Spice on Ice." It was about at the same time she, through the influence of a high school friend, converted to Pentecostal faith. Tacker was drawn to DeVilbiss' ministry. She listened to the "The Bible Answer Man" and attended his Bible studies that catered to entertainers. Tacker became one of his followers and regarded him as her pastor. Many show people listened to KILA. For some, Christian radio was a primary source of spiritual teaching and inspiration. Tacker's faith rendered her unpopular among the other skaters and dancers because she was outspoken about her faith and let it be known she intended to maintain a Christian lifestyle. The Bible, not peer pressure, would now govern

---

58. Mary DeVilbiss. Interview by author, October 1994. Mrs. DeVilbiss was the wife of Bob DeVilbiss. He held a Bible study on the Las Vegas strip from 1972–78 and was the Bible

59. Ibid.

her life and conduct. An example of her piety was her announced inten-tion to maintain virginity until marriage. It was what the Bible taught and she intended to do. During the course of the year, nine skaters in "Spice on Ice" also converted to Pentecostalism. This, however, created a division among the performers and, shortly thereafter, Tacker was fired from the show. She believed her dismissal was because of her faith.[60]

Ms. Tacker moved to the Flamingo Hotel where she worked her way up to the lead skater in "Playgirls on Ice." This show was hardly the setting where one would expect to find a virgin maiden of conservative religious persuasion. Other entertainers who converted eventually left the busi-ness, but she did not. By remaining, Tacker, like the bartender Kramer with his customers, believed she could be a missionary to the skaters and dancers.[61] In the minds of Pentecostals in other parts of the country, such a lifestyle was incongruent with the Spirit-filled life. But in Las Vegas, the rules were different. Janie Tacker did not grow up in the Bible Belt or come from a stereotypical evangelical home. She was born and raised in Las Vegas. While still a little girl, her father divorced her mother, and her mother supported her daughter by working as a cocktail waitress at the Tropicana Hotel.[62] As a Las Vegas native, Tacker did not have a bias against certain aspects of the entertainment industry. For her, dancing and partial nudity was part of the business. She read the Bible, interpreted its message, and developed a Christian lifestyle in the unique setting of the local culture.[63]

Denise McDonald was another member of the "Christ on Ice" dance team that performed at the Hacienda. She skated with Tacker in 1976 and later performed for several years at the Flamingo's "Razzle Dazzle." McDonald professed a born again experience in the late 1960s at a Billy Graham crusade in Garden Grove, California. One dimen-sion of McDonald's faith that differed from most of the others was that she performed topless, but never recognized a conflict between topless ice dancing and Christian piety. She also gravitated to the ministry of Reverend Bob DeVilbiss and attended his Bible studies. The Bible study

---

60. Jane Rammer. Interview by author, November 1994. Ms. Rammer was a skater on the Las Vegas strip in the late 1970s.

61. Ibid.

62. Ibid.

63. Ibid.

she frequented met on Saturday nights between shows.[64] The Christians she associated with did not criticize her for her occupation, but other non-religious performers did. They often observed that if she were really a Christian, she would not perform in those types of shows.[65]

Initially, McDonald's interest in charismatic faith was piqued by Hal Lindsay's book *The Late Great Planet Earth*.[66] Lindsey was a popular author and speaker among fundamentalists. At the time, Lindsay's book was a national bestseller, which claimed that the end of the age was imminent. The cold war was at its height, tensions in the Middle East were high, and the United States was undergoing a cultural revolution. Lindsey interpreted these events as fulfillment of biblical prophecy. McDonald was not alone in being captivated by end-time fervor, because an apocalyptic expectation was an integral part of charismatic faith. Denise McDonald was firmly convinced of the Bible's authority, but her acquiescence to biblical teaching was selective. She was a married woman and embraced a literal reading of Scripture as it pertained to a wife's submission to her husband. When asked how she reconciled topless dancing with faith, she replied that her "husband gave her permission."[67] For McDonald, biblical literalism applied to her marriage but not to her career as nude dancer. The experiences of McDonald and others involved in the revival on the Strip exemplify the interplay between Spirit and Word in Pentecostal exegesis. It was the Spirit that provided a sense of priority and application in their understanding of the biblical message.

While McDonald clearly compromised with her conscience, there is no doubt that she and other Strip converts were an important dimension of DeVilbiss' ministry, which appealed to all shades of faith. Unfortunately, his accomplishments were cut short by tragedy. On June 8, 1978, he and two of his children were killed in an automobile accident near Overton, Nevada. The overflow crowd that attended their funeral at Trinity Temple attested to his popularity. The church, which could seat one thousand people in overflow conditions, was packed and those who could not fit into the building stood outside.[68]

64. Mary DeVilbiss. Interview by author, October 1994.

65. Denise McDonald. Interview by author, November 1994. Ms. McDonald was an ice skater in various Las Vegas shows during the late 1970s.

66. Lindsey, *The Late Great Planet Earth*.

67. Denise McDonald. Interview by author, November 1994.

68. Melvin and Norma Steward. Interviewed by author, October 1994 and January 2002.

The emerging Pentecostal/Charismatic community of Las Vegas caught the attention of two nationally known evangelists. The first was a female, faith healing, ordained, Baptist minister named Katheryn Kuhlman. She gained a national following because of the purported miracles and many conversions that accompanied her meetings. She was also a flamboyant personality and dressed herself in dramatic flowing gowns. Her meetings were held throughout America, filling sports arenas and convention centers. Las Vegas Mayor Oran Gragson previously attended one of Kuhlman's crusades in Los Angeles, and he was so impressed he invited her to bring her ministry to his city. The Mayor was intrigued by the prospect of the notorious Las Vegas coming out for God. He was anxious for something more than simply another entertainment venue. In anticipation of her coming, he proclaimed May 3, 1975 to be Katheryn Kuhlman Day in Las Vegas.

She prepared for her coming by asking hundreds of people from across the nation to pray for the success of her debut in Las Vegas. Her evangelistic team swept into Vegas on a Saturday and overflowed the eight thousand seat convention center. *The Las Vegas Sun* said it "was the scene either of the greatest show on earth or the greatest story ever told."[69] On the night of the crusade people from all walks of life came out to hear the charismatic minister. The congregants included casino operators, prostitutes, entertainers, chorus girls, strippers, and black-jack dealers. There were representatives from all walks of life and religious affiliations.[70]

The "young woman of faith," (as she referred to herself) did not disappoint. Once she stepped on stage, a hard hitting salvation message was delivered, but she was careful not to exploit the reputation of sin city. In her words, "I don't think Las Vegas has as much sin as Los Angeles and New York. It's just publicized more."[71] During the course of the meeting upwards of two thousand people came forward to commit their lives to Christ. The charismatic evangelist also called out dozens within the audience and proclaimed God intended to heal them right then and there. A prayer was offered for divine intervention and dozen testified to miraculous healings. One was a totally deaf, self-proclaimed agnostic scientist

69. Anon. "Evangelist Kuhlman Draws LV Multitude." *Las Vegas Sun*, May 4, 1975.

70. Warner. "Remembering Evangelist Kathryn Kuhlman."

71. "Famed evangelist comes to Vegas by 'God's will." *Las Vegas Review Journal*, May 3, 1975.

who exclaimed that his hearing was supernaturally restored. That same night he professed a conversion to Christianity.[72]

Emotions ran high throughout the evening. Perhaps representative of those in attendance was the testimony of one uniformed security guard. As a soloist sang an old gospel song, there were tears streaming down the guard's face. Forgetting he was on duty, he lifted both hands and joined in singing *It Is Well With My Soul*: "My sin, oh, the bliss of this glorious thought: My sin not the part but the whole is nailed to the cross, and I bear it no more, Praise the Lord, praise the Lord, 0 my soul!"[73]

Kathryn Kuhlman only came to Las Vegas once, but she left her mark on the city. Her ministry here demonstrated the openness to and vitality of the Pentecostalist message in the entertainment capital of North America. Thousands of Pentecostal people can still remember where they were and what they were doing on February 26, 1976 when they received the news over the networks and wire services that the famed evangelist had died. Her visit to Las Vegas turned out to be one of her last meetings.

It was a little more than two years later that the dean of American evangelists, Billy Graham held the first of two Las Vegas crusades. Both were well received. His first was in February of 1978. The five-day crusade broke city attendance records, and thousands came forward to accept Jesus Christ as personal Lord and Savior. The first crusade was so successful he made a rare return visit in November 1980. Again, the crusade was a numerical success, as thousands responded to the appeal of the popular evangelist.[74] It was also significant that in 1978 Graham chose Trinity Temple, a Pentecostal church, to host his School of Evangelism and crusade headquarters.[75] Graham chose Las Vegas from among more than eight thousand invitations. The churches, politicians, and local business people welcomed him with open arms. *The Las Vegas Review Journal* reported one hundred of the city's 115 Protestant churches actively supported the crusade.[76] Mel Peckrul, pastor at the First Baptist Church and

72. Warner, "Remembering Evangelist Kathryn Kuhlman," *Pentecostal Evangel*, February 2003, 29.

73. Ibid.

74. Kastelic. "Records Set During Nevada Crusade," *Las Vegas Review Journal*, 12 June, 1980.

75. Melvin and Norma Steward. Interviewed by author, October 1994 and January 2002. Rev. Steward pastored Trinity from 1974–84.

76. Fredrick, "Billy Graham Crusade Off to a Local Start," *Las Vegas Review Journal*, September 17, 1977.

patriarch of valley pastors, said he had seen nothing like it in his seventeen years of Las Vegas service. Griffith United Methodist Minister, Gil Gray, called the crusade a "source of revitalization."[77]

Enthusiasm among the laity was evidenced by the recruitment of a 1,300-voice choir comprised of lay people from local churches.[78] Local politicians demonstrated enthusiasm, also. Mayor Bill Briare invited Graham to speak at the Governor's and Mayor's Prayer Breakfast the day before the crusade began.[79] Briare addressed the prayer breakfast crowd and called the Graham meetings "the beginning of a spiritual super bowl."[80] Governor Mike O'Callaghan and Mayor Briare both attended the opening night service.[81] The Las Vegas Convention and Visitors Authority got involved too, voting for the promotional agency to pick up the $4,000 tab for setting up and cleaning up the convention center where the crusade was held.[82] They recognized that the national publicity attached to endorsing Billy Graham helped soften the city's reputation.

Billy Graham was well received. Both the *Las Vegas Review Journal* and *Las Vegas Sun* provided favorable coverage. During the days of the event, both papers consistently provided front-page coverage. Graham declared he was amazed at "the reception he and his team received."[83] Crusade attendance was beyond all expectations. On opening night, about 13,000 people filled the Las Vegas Convention Center. An overflow area had to be opened to accommodate the throng.[84] The *Review-Journal* reported Graham "packed the Convention Center like it has

77. Fredrick, "Graham Crusade Unites Local Churches," *Las Vegas Review Journal*, January 29, 1978.

78. Fredrick, "Graham Choir Director Talks," *Las Vegas Review Journal*, February 3, 1978.

79. Fredrick, "Graham Crusade Unites Local Churches," *Las Vegas Review Journal*, January 29, 1978.

80. Fredrick, "Graham Tells of Spiritual Fire," *Las Vegas Review Journal*, January 31, 1978.

81. Fredrick, "Overflow Crowd Hears Graham," *Las Vegas Review Journal*, February 2, 1978.

82. Breger, "Authority Votes 'Freebie' For Evangelistic Crusade," *Las Vegas Review Journal*, September 28, 1977.

83. Newburn, "Graham Surprised By Las Vegas' Response," *Las Vegas Sun*, February 6, 1978.

84. Fredrick, "Overflow Crowd Hears Graham," *Las Vegas Review Journal*, February 2, 1978.

never been packed before.[85] The official statistics provided by the Billy Graham Evangelistic Association reported a total attendance of 63,000 people with 3,144 conversions during the five-day crusade.[86] Graham understood the unique nature of Las Vegas and adapted his method and message to the local culture. He was conscious of the town's reputation and the local desire to project a more wholesome image. Graham took advantage of opportunities to downplay the city's sinful reputation. He stressed Las Vegas was no more sinful than many other cities by saying: "The Scriptures teach us that everyone is in great spiritual need. We have all sinned and fallen short of the glory of God. I didn't come here to condemn Las Vegas."[87] Graham was careful not to condemn casino gambling. He noted that it was not specifically prohibited in the Bible, but there were biblical principles that could be applied to the subject. When asked specifically about gambling, Graham replied, "The greatest center of gambling is Wall Street."[88] He held a special rally for casino workers in which he spiritualized gambling. Graham told them "the greatest gamble in the world is the gamble a man makes with his own soul."[89]

The famous evangelist also recognized the strong Mormon presence in the valley and was careful not to offend them. Officially, the Mormons were neutral about Graham coming to town. However, the evangelist down-played the lukewarm reaction of the Church of Jesus Christ of Latter Day Saints and declared he was confident some Mormons would attend.[90] Even though he said, "I do not accept the teachings of the Mormon Church," he also publicly stated some of his best friends were Mormon and granted the possibility that a Mormon may be "born again" and still remain a Mormon.[91]

85. Fredrick, "Graham Crusade Packs Center for 3rd Night," *Las Vegas Review Journal*, February 4, 1978.

86. Billy Graham Evangelistic Association. Official statistical records of crusades from 1976–82. Field Ministries: P.O. Box 9313, Minneapolis, MN.

87. Galatz, "Graham Arrives in Las Vegas 'To Proclaim Gospel,'" *Las Vegas Sun*, January 31, 1978.

88. Fredrick, "Graham Expects Mormons at Crusade," *Las Vegas Review Journal*, January 31, 1978.

89. Ibid.

90. Galatz, Karen. "Graham Arrives in Las Vegas 'To Proclaim Gospel,'" *Las Vegas Sun*, January 31, 1978.

91. Fredrick, "Graham Expects Mormons at Crusade," *Las Vegas Review Journal*, January 31, 1978.

Graham and his evangelistic team's strategists recognized the appeal of celebrities to the citizenry of Las Vegas. Country singer Johnny Cash and his wife June Carter were present opening night as was the Lawrence Welk Show's lead singer Norma Zimmer. Cash sang two songs and told the crowd Jesus Christ was the Lord of his life. The entertainer pledged to attend all five nights of the crusade. The second night featured pop singer B. J. Thomas. Thomas told of his past experience with drug addiction and testified how his faith in Jesus Christ salvaged both his personal and professional life. He sang before a youth night audience of nearly 12,000.[92]

Las Vegas was a twenty-four-hour town, so Graham had to adapt his ministry to fit the schedules of those who worked on the Strip. At the suggestion of Strip chaplain Jim Reid, Graham held a special service at 3:00 a.m. to accommodate work shifts of entertainers and gaming dealers. About 1,000 people attended and forty-three people responded to the invitation to receive Christ. The inquirers included a Moslem belly dancer, three showgirls, seven cocktail waitresses, four keno runners, a bartender, a craps dealer, and a man who claimed to be a homosexual hotel worker.[93]

The Graham crusade's success was an important contributor to the Las Vegas charismatic awakening that occurred in the 1970s and 1980s. A key to Graham's appeal was his ability to adapt his message to the local culture. As Revivalist scholar William McLoughlin observed, "A great deal of Graham's popularity . . . stems from the fact that he purposely avoids controversy on divisive issues."[94]

In 1984, Reverend Greg Massanari organized a new church named Cornerstone Christian Fellowship. There was an interesting relationship between Sahara Hotel owner, Paul Lowden, and Cornerstone. Lowden, a nominal Catholic, converted to the Pentecostal faith and developed a personal relationship with Pastor Massanari. Lowden provided space at the Sahara Hotel for the fledgling church to conduct worship services. The hotel owner often talked with Pastor Greg about the conflict between his religion and hotel business. One occasion for such a discussion was the Redd Foxx Show, which was laced with profanity and explicit sexual humor. Lowden almost decided against bringing Foxx to the Sahara. The issue turned on a personal plea by Foxx's mother who was a devout

92. McVey, "A Matter of Love," *Las Vegas Sun*, February 3, 1978.

93. Fredrick, "Crusade Tiring for Graham," *Las Vegas Review Journal*, February 2, 1978.

94. McLoughlin, *Billy Graham: Revivalist in a Secular Age*, 1960, 93.

Christian and concerned about the salvation of her son. Upon learning that Paul Lowden was a professing Christian, she called and urged him to bring the show to his hotel because he might be the one person who could bring her son to repentance. Redd Foxx did perform at the Sahara.[95] Lowden justified the apparent contradiction between the church and the casino's sponsorship of gambling and alcohol as cultural matters using the writings of the apostle Paul as a guideline.[96]

Local churches, backstage Bible studies, KILA radio, and the Billy Graham Crusades were all components of the Las Vegas revival. Some characteristics of the local revitalization were common to other revivals, but some things were distinctive to the local phenomenon. One might assume converts immediately left their questionable means of livelihood upon conversion to charismatic Christianity. Such was not the case. In every case examined, the revival converts continued their professions on the Strip while remaining deeply devoted to their faith. Over the course of time, most did feel "led" to change careers, but some never recognized a contradiction between their work and church teachings.

It might also be assumed that the Strip converts experienced condemnation by their pastors or churches because of their professions, but again, such was not the case. The churches and ministers in Las Vegas adapted their message to the city's distinct culture. Only one entertainer recalled a pastor who preached against involvement in show business, and his ministry quickly folded.[97] Surprisingly, most of those interviewed commented on the sometimes intense discrimination they experienced from their professional colleagues who were not connected with the charismatic awakening. The unconverted were the ones with inflexible positions about how a Christian should live.

One might think a Las Vegas revival would attract converts into more liberal, less pietistic churches, but this was not the case. There was no evidence of the Strip revival converts joining liberal churches. Some initially gravitated to independent Bible study groups and almost all eventually ended up in conservative, Bible-centered, Pentecostal or

95. Greg Massanari. Interview by author, October 1994. Rev. Massanari pastored another charismatic church in Las Vegas (Christian Life Community) during the 1980s. He was also a close personal acquaintance with several in leadership at Calvary Chapel/ Dove Ministries.

96. Ibid.

97. Denise McDonald. Interview by author, November 1994.

charismatic churches. The converts were selective biblical literalists, and they looked for churches that emphasized Bible-centered and Spirit ener-gized forms of Christianity.

The revival on the Strip did not fit the mold of the "control theory" of popular religion. This theory maintains that America's industrial and economic leaders had traditionally encouraged religious involvement, because they saw religion as a means of social control. Paul Johnson was one noted historian who challenged this theory. He believed religious re-vivals in American history were grassroots movements that help converts gain self control.[98] One Las Vegas hotel owner, Paul Lowden, did convert, but he did not attempt to control his work force in any demonstrable way. The only sense in which the Strip revival fit a control theory was that religious belief became a means of "self-control."

The Strip revival corresponded with other American revivals in some ways. Religious historian Nathan Hatch believed American revivals were typically grass roots, populist movements. According to Hatch, they were experiential, localized, and democratically oriented. The revival on the Strip shared much in common with the nineteenth century revivals Hatch studied. They were led by charismatic personalities who had the ability to connect with everyday people. Their leaders were not highly educated but were able to relate their message to the popular culture.[99] The Las Vegas revival was not an isolated episode but should be viewed in the larger context of the national awakening during this period. The 1960s and 1970s were the years of the Jesus movement loosely connected with the hippy or counter-culture activities of the same time frame. Charismatics emphasized eschatology and the ministry of the Holy Spirit in the present age. It was during this time that television and radio evange-lists become media personalities. Jimmy Swaggart, Jim and Tammy Faye Bakker's PTL Club, and the 700 Club with Pat Robertson were prominent. The Las Vegas revival was probably best understood as the local version of a national charismatic phenomenon.

Oral interviews indicate no single over-arching reason for people's conversions. For some there was a need for a moral foundation for their lives. For others there was an acute sense of guilt for past actions. It is in-teresting to note that several of the showgirls interviewed acknowledged

98. Johnson, *A Shopkeeper's Millennium.*

99. Hatch, *The Democratization of American Christianity*, 221. Rice, "Minister to the Strip," *Nevadan*, October 6, 1974, 30–31.

having an abortion in order to stay physically attractive and not miss time on the job. They felt compelled to terminate pregnancies to continue their careers. Their faith provided the spiritual means with which they could absolve personal guilt.

The Las Vegas revival was an exception to a commonly held understanding of Pentecostal Christianity. Pentecostals, often defined as intransigent, narrow minded, and inflexible in matters concerning appropriate Christian behavior, may be the case in other parts of America, but the Las Vegas revival manifested a remarkable capacity to adapt the message to the local culture. Las Vegas Pentecostals understood well the New Testament Pauline dictum, "To the Jews I became like a Jew, and to win the Jews I have become all things to all men so that by all possible means I might save some" (1 Cor 9:20).

7

The Rise and Fall of Camelot

There was a little girl who had a little curl right in the middle of her forehead, and when she was good she was very good, but when she was bad, she was horrid.

THIS OLD NURSERY RHYME appropriately captures the dynamics of one of Las Vegas' most celebrated congregations. For a time during the 1980s it embodied many qualities that characterized Pentecostalism's capacity to succeed. It had cultural relevance, a targeted audience, interesting preaching, contemporary music, and charismatic leadership. However, it soon descended as rapidly as it had previously ascended. Las Vegas Pentecostalism fell victim to poor infrastructure, authoritarian leadership, moral compromise, and egomania. Once upon a time, this is what happened.

American society was dramatically reordered during the 1960s and 1970s. Religion played a major role in this cultural chaos. This was the era of the Jesus movement and the heyday of televangelism. Pentecostalism influenced both of these fresh expressions of evangelical Christianity. Calvary Chapel in Costa Mesa, California, and its Pentecostal pastor, helped lead the spiritual awakening in southern California. Thousands of young people searched for spiritual expression outside the established mainstream churches. There was a genuine interest in the person and message of Jesus, but not the one found in traditional Christianity. A version of this brand of Pentecostal faith rose like a phoenix in Las Vegas.

This quest for a contemporary (they would argue more authentic) expression of faith set aside many of the trappings of the established Christian church. These believers were not interested in church buildings, robed choirs, Rogers' organs, or seminary-trained ministers. They placed little value on tradition or a liturgical form of worship. Theirs was a post-modern formation of faith that placed little confidence in long held absolutes and institutional authority. Instead, they emphasized a spirituality grounded in a personal relationship with God. Their faith was anchored by personal experience instead of an agreed upon, inherited creed.

There were several well-known entertainers who converted to this new brand of popular Christianity. Some rock and roll stars like Barry McGuire and B. J. Thomas embraced Pentecostal Christianity. Even Bob Dylan, a Jew, briefly embraced the faith and recorded an album, entitled *Slow Train*, with strong Christian overtones. A new brand of Christian music was also born. Youthful musicians who converted formed Christian bands and held Woodstock-like music festivals with thousands in attendance. It became chic to be a Christian in the format of this contemporary, post-modern spirituality.

Another major force in this new kind of Christianity was the emergence of televangelism. Prime-time religion reached a mass market through the ministries of such personalities as Jimmy Swaggart and Jim and Tammy Bakker. Both Swaggart and the Bakkers held credentials with the Assemblies of God, the largest Pentecostal organization in North America. Pat Robertson, who brought a new rendition of Pentecostalism into the homes of Americans from coast to coast, was a self-proclaimed charismatic. He held to a Pentecostal theology that emphasized an experiential encounter with the Holy Spirit. Televangelists claimed a viewing audience numbering in the millions, and staggering amounts of money poured into their coffers.[1] The televangelists' genius for presentation and their visceral connection with multitudes of Americans also found a receptive audience in Las Vegas. KILA, a local Christian radio station, claimed a large listening audience. Its popularity was evidenced by the amount of money donations that came in to support its broadcasts and by ratings analysis.[2] Both the Jesus movement and televangelism were essential ingredients in the rise of a large and influential congregation in Las Vegas. This phenomenon represented a local manifestation of a larger restructuring of religion in America.

This expression of Christian faith became institutionalized as churches organized around new non-traditional converts. One of the hot

1. Shepard Charles, *Forgiven*, 155–160.

2. Jack French. Interview by author, March 1992. Mr. French was owner and manager of KILA radio station established in Las Vegas in 1972.

spots for this new formation of faith was Southern California. In 1965, an obscure Foursquare pastor named Chuck Smith (who later came to be known simply as Pastor Chuck), moved to Costa Mesa to lead a small independent church known as Calvary Chapel. Under his ministry the congregation grew at a weekly rate of 5 percent! An influx of longhaired hippies inundated his church.[3] Pastor Chuck had the wisdom to welcome them even though they did not fit the mold of traditional church members. His acceptance of these counter-culture youth encouraged many to come, and soon his congregation swelled into the hundreds. Within a few years, Calvary Chapel was a mega-church numbering thousands in weekly attendance.

Calvary Chapel's ministry was characterized by Pastor Chuck's verse-by-verse style of biblical exposition. Smith also introduced contemporary music with weekly Saturday night concerts that appealed to thousands of youthful seekers who thronged his church. The phenomenon of Calvary Chapel Costa Mesa was important because the man who established Calvary Chapel Las Vegas, Pat Walsh, was at one time involved in the Costa Mesa church. Walsh incorporated many aspects of Calvary Chapel Costa Mesa into his Las Vegas "Calvary Chapel." The style that was so successful in California brought similar results in southern Nevada.

Pat Walsh was raised a Catholic, but as an adult he joined an Assemblies of God church in Costa Mesa. Later, he migrated across town to the ministry of Chuck Smith at Calvary Chapel. Walsh had no formal theological training and was not ordained by any national denomination. His professional background was in business management and marketing. For a time, Walsh served as Southern California area marketing director for McDonald's fast-foods restaurants.[4] His prowess would later factor into the success of his church planting in Las Vegas.

After leaving Costa Mesa, Walsh relocated to Redding, California. While there, he organized and founded a Calvary Chapel. The work in Redding did not flourish numerically under the leadership of Walsh, so his group later merged with another congregation, Little Country Church. In less than a decade, it grew to approximately two thousand

3. Balmer, *Mine Eyes Have Seen the Glory*, 12–29.

4. Pat Walsh. Interview by author, November 2000 and January 2001. Rev. Walsh was the founding pastor of Calvary Chapel Las Vegas and continued as its head into the early 1990s.

five-hundred members. Walsh was instrumental in the church's founding, but was not the one who led it to its zenith.[5]

Walsh again moved, this time to Los Alamos, New Mexico, where he founded another Calvary Chapel. Both the church in Redding and Los Alamos were established with the blessing of Chuck Smith and the mother church in Costa Mesa, California. Since Calvary Chapel did not regard itself as a denomination, there was no formal process by which a new work would gain official endorsement. The permission to begin a new work was really nothing more than an expression of approval by Pastor Chuck. In early 1980, Walsh moved to Las Vegas with the dream of establishing still another Calvary Chapel. He claimed, "the Lord spoke directly to me" in asking him to move to Las Vegas. Conversations with Walsh revealed that many of his decisions were based on a subjective sense of what he believed the Lord was personally revealing. After three months of living in the city and praying for the "Lord's strategy," the vision became a reality. On May 8, 1980, Walsh began holding services with an initial congregation of twenty-seven adults and twenty-four children. Their first church home was Bunker Mortuary on Las Vegas Boulevard.[6]

Walsh was something of a "Bapticostal" in that he emphasized biblical teaching in Baptist fashion. Conservative Baptists hold to Scripture as the rule of faith and practice. For Baptists, Scripture was the only reliable medium of communication between God and man. His style and delivery emulated that of Pastor Chuck in Costa Mesa. Walsh incorporated the moving of the Spirit in a more Pentecostal style of faith. In this respect, he was more Pentecostal than Baptist. He was heavily influenced by the Baptist concept of the Word and a Pentecostal interpretation of the Spirit. His theology on this point developed while attending Calvary Chapel in Costa Mesa, California, and was similar to that of Pastor Chuck's.

While there were certainly deep ideological convictions that shaped his ministry style and content, it was the acumen of Walsh's marketing expertise that helped popularize his fledgling congregation.[7] Walsh tapped into the counterculture mentality so prevalent among young adults at

---

5. Ibid.

6. Ibid.

7. Ted Ramy. Interview by author, November 2001. Rev. Ramy came to Dove Ministries in the late 1980s and followed John Perenti to Meadows Fellowship. Ted pastored Meadows when Perenti resigned.

the time. The music of Calvary Chapel Las Vegas was a trendy form of Christian rock and folk music. Piano, guitars, and drums were the instruments of choice, and vocalists, who wore jeans and casual shirts, often sported long hair. Walsh utilized the services of some of the best musicians in town. Sometimes a brass section was part of the praise team, and for a time there was a harpist. Other strategic techniques that proved successful included the showing of popular Christian films and importing nationally known speakers to address the congregation. Drama was also used as an effective means of communication. The biblical teaching was well presented. As a preacher, Walsh exhibited a talent for presenting his message in a way that gained popular acceptance. One former member commented, "It always spoke directly to some issue in my life."[8] Walsh's ability to appeal to the personal interests of his followers combined with his compelling verse-by-verse exposition of the Bible proved to be a winning recipe for numerical growth. Within one year, the congregation grew to approximately 200.[9] There was a certain sense of spiritual superiority that characterized some of the congregation. They were aggressive proselytes of members from other evangelical and Pentecostal churches. For instance, members of Calvary Chapel sometimes waited in the parking lot outside Trinity Temple and passed out leaflets to openly solicited adherents of that church to leave Trinity and come join them at Calvary Chapel.[10] This angered the pastors of other churches but reflected Walsh's aggressive marketing strategy.

In 1981, the congregation of Calvary Chapel leased an old auto parts building in downtown Las Vegas where they leased commercial property. Their new address was 900 South Las Vegas Boulevard. Part of the appeal of Calvary Chapel was that it did not own property and did not worship in a traditional church building. The anti-establishment generation to which they appealed preferred the non-traditionalism of leased commercial space. An unadorned church facility was another

8. Round Robin. Interview by author with several former members of Calvary Chapel/Dove Ministries, August 2000. It included Joe and Bonnie Roush, Duke and Judy Redburn, and Taffy Lakatos.

9. John Michaels. Interview by author, December 2001. Rev. Michaels was an associate pastor with Pat Walsh from 1982–86 at Calvary Chapel/Dove Ministries. He left Dove Ministries to start a second Calvary Chapel work in Las Vegas.

10. Melvin and Norma Steward. Interviews by author, October 1994 and January 2002. Rev.Steward pastored Trinity from 1974–1984.

similarity between Calvary Chapel, Las Vegas and Calvary Chapel in Costa Mesa, California.

Later that same year, Walsh began hiring associates to help with the rapidly expanding ministry of Calvary Chapel. John Perenti was brought on staff as a pastor. Perenti came without formal theological training. His only previous church leadership experience was limited to an assistant's role at Boulder City, Nevada, Christian Center. The church in Boulder City was affiliated with the Foursquare denomination. He came to Calvary Chapel from the leading local Christian radio station, KILA, where he worked as a disk jockey. Perenti was also a talented musician who previously performed with a Christian music group. Walsh recognized Perenti's charisma, talent, and ability to verbally communicate.[11]

In 1982, Walsh hired John Michaels to join the staff. He, too, was without professional theological training or experience. Michaels possessed a college degree from Florida State University, but it was in meteorology not pastoral ministry. After moving to Las Vegas he worked for the Department of Energy and was an active layman at First Baptist Church of Las Vegas.[12] Walsh's nonconformist style was exemplified in his selection of pastoral staff. He not only chose individuals without formal training for the ministry, but also refused to identify them as assistant pastors. In Walsh's view, the only qualifications to be a minister were that "a person is born again by the Spirit of God and recognized the calling of God." This opinion was based on Jesus Christ's selection of ordinary, unknown, uneducated people including fishermen and a tax collector. Walsh's handpicked ministers considered themselves pastors on equal footing with Pat Walsh. This removal of hierarchical standing fit well with the egalitarian mindset of the "question authority" generation to which Walsh appealed so strongly.

In light of comments by church members and those in leadership with Walsh, it was more of a feigned egalitarianism than the real thing. The board lacked decision-making power and their opinions were not solicited when he made pastoral staff choices. A conversation with a board member who served at the time revealed that the church board only served to confirm the decisions Walsh personally made. "We were just yes men who were expected to rubber-stamp whatever Pat Walsh decided

---

11. Pat Walsh. Interviews by author, November 2000 and January 2001.

12. John Michaels. Interview by author, December 2001.

to do."[13] Walsh liked to project the image of shared leadership, but in fact he controlled every major decision.

The congregation continued to grow, and in 1983, the church again outgrew its facilities. This time it leased a complex of new buildings at 2500 West Washington. While no official church records exist, former pastors, parishioners, and local newspapers all reported the church grew at an amazing rate. Walsh claimed it doubled in size every five months for approximately six years.[14]

In October 1985, the church relocated once more as booming attendance forced leaders to purchase an old shopping center at Rancho and Bonanza. Walsh sought private financing because banks were reluctant to lend to churches. Surprisingly, he secured part of the needed money from gamblers Ted Binion, who loaned Walsh $40,000 and Puggy Pearson who loaned him $60,000. Perhaps Binion was motivated, in part, by a personal fondness for employees who were members of the church. Duke Redburn had known Benny Binion since 1953. Duke originally met Benny as a nineteen-year-old marine who visited Joe Brown's Horseshoe Club. Duke eventually retired from the marines in 1973 and came to work as a dealer.[15] Another Horseshoe employee who joined Calvary Chapel was Kent Nottingham. Nottingham moved to town in 1974 and worked in the casino as a floor man and later became a pit boss. Nottingham was also actively involved at Calvary Chapel. There were a number of Binion's Horseshoe employees who attended the church. One former employee speculated that Nottingham used his position at the Horseshoe as a way of encouraging other employees to attend the church. Perhaps they would gain some advantage in the workplace if they went to their boss's church.[16] It was Nottingham who initially approached Ted Binion about loaning money to the church. Clearly, his friendship with Binion helped secure the loan. It was shortly thereafter that Nottingham left the casino and made a surprising career change from dealer to pastor. He became director of the schools at Calvary Chapel.[17]

---

13. Duke Redburn. Interview by author, November 2001. Mr. Redburn was a Board member of Calvary Chapel Las Vegas from 1986–88.

14. Pat Walsh. Interviews by author, November 2000 and January 2001.

15. Duke Redburn. Interview by author, November 2001.

16. Ibid.

17. Ibid.

The growing congregation developed other ministries to comple-
ment its Sunday services. A Christian school was established which included elementary grades through high school. Those who were able paid
tuition, but the church's general fund provided scholarships for families
who could not afford the full cost.[18] A peak enrollment of 265 students
was reached by 1985.[19] Calvary Chapel also established an adult education program under the name River of Life Bible School. Its purpose was
to train men and women for ministry.

There were several other ministry enterprises launched by Walsh's
Calvary Chapel. The church opened a bookstore that recorded gross sales
of $250,000 in 1985. Calvary Chapel also created a business called the
Heavenly Travel Agency. The agency's stated purpose was to facilitate
and profit from the travel plans of church members. It helped organize
Christian-oriented group tours of the Holy Land. Walsh personally used
Heavenly Travel in organizing six such tours.[20]

Calvary Chapel became prominent in the city, so the church's leadership exploited its high profile and sought to evangelize the business
community with prayer breakfasts every other Thursday. The prayer
group named itself B.L.E.S.S. God, an acronym for "Business Leaders and
Executives Seeking to Serve God."[21] On two occasions, the church leased
Wet'n'Wild water park for nights of Christian fun and entertainment. The
evenings were augmented by water baptisms of recent converts in one of
the pools at the park.[22] Other outreach ministries included an emergency
hotline, a drug recovery program, and a team of church members who
visited hospitals and convalescent centers.[23] Walsh's genius for marketing
created a popular ministry that appealed to the local taste for things fun,
relevant, and creative. Word spread about the phenomenon of Calvary

18. Dennis Lee. Interview by author, November 2001. Rev. Lee was a member of
Calvary Chapel since the early 1980s and eventually pastored Hallelujah Fellowship.

19. Pat Walsh. Interview by author, November 2000 and January 2001. Rev. Walsh
was the founding pastor of Calvary Chapel Las Vegas and continued as its head into the
early 1990s.

20. Ibid.

21. Weier, "Business Group Puts God on Agenda," *Las Vegas Review Journal*, June
23, 1986.

22. Beall, "Dove Ministries Conducts Baptism on Las Vegas Strip," *Las Vegas Review
Journal*, August 24, 1986.

23. Weier, "Pastors at Las Vegas Church Step Down," *Las Vegas Review Journal*,
November 24, 1987.

Chapel Las Vegas, and Walsh received numerous guest-speaker invitations. He was given the use of a parishioner's privately owned plane, and a pilot within the congregation flew him to destinations across the country to keep pace with his growing list of special engagements.

By 1985, the weekly attendance averaged 5,000 people.[24] It took six services on Sunday to accommodate the crowds that gathered in a 750-seat auditorium for services. As the congregation grew, it began to gain national attention through the Christian television and radio media. In 1985, the 700 Club, hosted by Pat Robertson, identified Calvary Chapel Las Vegas as one of the fastest-growing churches in America. Stories about the church appeared in several religious periodicals, and Jim and Tammy Bakker's PTL Club dedicated an entire program to recognize Walsh's church. Campus Crusade for Christ, a national organization geared to college students, invited him to be part of a symposium consisting of leaders of the ten fastest growing churches in America.[25] Walsh used the success of Calvary Chapel Las Vegas as a springboard for two evangelistic crusades in South Korea. The dream behind the trips to Korea was to establish new churches there that would be an extension of his ministry in Las Vegas.[26]

Pat Walsh, like some popular televangelists of the same period, won praise for offering a good-humored, relaxed presentation of the gospel. Laurence Moore, in *Selling God*, noted that the success of late twentieth-century televangelists depended in large measure upon repackaging their message into an appealing imitation of the entertainment media. He praised them for an effective, sincere presentation of a distinct version of Christianity.[27] Walsh also developed a sophisticated program with great appeal to his contemporary audience.

Under Walsh's pastoral leadership, Calvary Chapel did not require its adherents' membership, and there was a come-as-you-are open invitation. Worshipers did not have to observe a dress code or meet any specific criteria to feel welcome at church. As one former member recalled, "There was such an atmosphere of love and acceptance. Everyone was so friendly and accepting of each other."[28] On certain issues there was not

24. Ibid.
25. Pat Walsh. Interview by author, November 2000 and January 2001.
26. Dennis Lee. Interview by author, November 2001.
27. Moore, *Selling God*, 3–4.
28. Round Robin. Interview by author with several former members of Calvary

much emphasis upon a specific code of behavior. Walsh left decisions of an appropriate lifestyle as a matter of personal conscience. For instance, there was a well-known Strip performer who was a practicing lesbian (homosexuality being a serious sin among evangelical Christians), who sang weekly on stage at the church.[29] Walsh appeared to make exceptions for individuals who were especially talented or, in some way, attracted more people to the church. He argued that it was the Holy Spirit who prioritized and stylized his ministry.[30] Whatever the motivation, he had a knack for framing the gospel to fit the local culture.

While Walsh was open-minded on certain social issues, he was much more legalistic on others. For instance, he once published and distributed a tract setting forth the church's view of divorce and remarriage.[31] He was adamant that Christians were not permitted to divorce and remarry under any circumstance. One member recalled that a fellow parishioner who decided to remarry was not allowed to hold the ceremony at the church, no staff pastor was allowed to perform the marriage, and her friends in the church were not allowed to attend the ceremony.[32] He was not guided by tradition, denominational affiliation, or consistent biblical literalism. Walsh was eclectic and self-serving in his enforcement of behavioral expectations.

The Pentecostal emphasis upon the moving of the Spirit typically manifested itself at the end of the formal worship service when members gathered around the altar for a special prayer. These were called "afterglow" services and were always led by the recognized pastors. During the afterglow, there would be prayer for the sick. Congregants claimed that many miraculous healings occurred. They also encouraged people to seek a special spiritual blessing. It was common for individuals to speak in other tongues or to be "slain in the Spirit." This term described someone falling prostrate in an ecstatic state. There were accounts of individuals being "drunk" in the Spirit, that is, they could not walk straight after an ecstatic experience during the altar service. At other times, there would

---

Chapel/Dove Ministries, August 2000. Group included Joe and Bonnie Roush; Duke and Judy Redburn; and Taffy Lakatos.

29. Ted Ramy. Interview by author, November 2001.

30. Pat Walsh. Interview by author, November 2000 and January 2001.

31. Walsh, *Marriage, Divorce & Remarriage*.

32. Round Robin. Interview by author with several former members of Calvary Chapel/Dove Ministries, August 2000.

be prophetic utterances or personal guidance believed to be inspired by the Holy Spirit.[33] Pat Walsh's success in Las Vegas not only made him a popular pastor in Nevada, but also inspired him to plant other churches throughout the Southwest and as far East as Boston. Walsh frequently left Calvary Chapel Las Vegas in the care of his handpicked associates while he planted new congregations in Kingman, Arizona; Lake Havasu, Arizona; Reno, Nevada; St. George, Utah; Richmond, Virginia; and Boston, Massachusetts.

Walsh gave great freedom and latitude to his co-pastors, but he failed to take into account the possible usurpation of power. With Walsh away so much, the other pastors became rivals for Walsh's Las Vegas flock. This was not surprising, because each had a congregation that he was re-sponsible for at a particular Sunday service. Not surprisingly, the separate pastors began to feel that these worshipers were their own.[34]

Another contributing factor was a growing uneasiness concerning Walsh's ethics.[35] The seeds of division, which eventually split the church, began to germinate within the leadership. Walsh was innovative and non-traditional in his leadership style, but his non-conventional approach to ministry created an environment without adequate checks and balances. According to Walsh, the pastors left in charge of the Las Vegas work be-gan posturing to take over the church while he was ministering in other places. Walsh saw himself primarily as a church-planter, thus, he main-tained, it was only a matter of time before he left Las Vegas altogether in favor of some new mission field.[36] Others, however, wondered whether Walsh had any intention of releasing his control over the work in Las Vegas.[37] Whatever Walsh's actual motives were, a rivalry developed be-tween John Michaels and John Perenti.

Walsh came to believe it necessary for one individual to be in charge of the whole church because he was away so much. He hoped the ap-pointment of one leader would resolve the strained relations among the pastoral staff, but the tension only increased when Walsh named Perenti the senior pastor. There never was a congregational vote or any other

33. Ibid.

34. Ibid.

35. John Michaels. Interview by author, December 2001.

36. Pat Walsh. Interview by author, November 2000 and January 2001.

37. John Michaels. Interview by author, December 2001.

democratic process in his selection.[38] John Michaels did not support Walsh's choice of Perenti, and it was only a matter of time before Michaels would resign.

Calvary Chapel's influence peaked in 1986. According to Walsh, the growing influence of Calvary Chapel Las Vegas only confused the relationship between the church in Las Vegas and Calvary Chapel Costa Mesa. There never was a binding alliance between the two, so Walsh used his prominence to establish the ministry in Las Vegas with its own name and identity. This seemed the perfect way to distinguish the Las Vegas work and yet retain a positive relationship with Costa Mesa. Walsh changed the name of Calvary Chapel Las Vegas to Dove Ministries and formed a corporation called Dove International. Walsh appointed himself president of Dove International, which served as an umbrella organization over the church. Former members recall that the announcement of a name change was simply made to the congregation one Sunday morning. Neither the members nor the church board were involved in the decision.[39] This created some unrest within the congregation, because many members felt secure in the church's association with Calvary Chapel Costa Mesa. At that time, Dove Ministries averaged several thousand in weekly attendance and there were nine pastors on staff. The church's national reputation was at its zenith.[40]

Walsh also renamed River of Life Bible College to Dove Christian College. Walsh envisioned it becoming a fully accredited college offering majors in a number of different disciplines. Schools such as Biola College and Oral Roberts University were examples of what Dove Christian College aspired to emulate![41] A former UNLV basketball star, Lonnie Wright, was the college's director of development, and he approached UNLV basketball Coach Jerry Tarkanian about partnering with the university. Wright wanted Dove Christian College to develop a basketball program that would serve as a feeder to the nationally prominent basketball team at UNLV.[42] The dream was big and might have been fulfilled

38. Round Robin. Interview by author with several former members of Calvary Chapel/Dove Ministries, August 2000.

39. Ibid.

40. *Calvary Chapel Organizational Sheet*, 4.

41. Pappa. "Christian College Mulls Broad Series of Courses," *Las Vegas Sun*, February 9, 1987.

42. Ibid.

had it not been for problems looming on the horizon. Calvary Chapel/ Dove began to implode just a year later, and the reality of a full-fledged Christian college never actually materialized.

There is an interesting parallel between the UNLV basketball team's rapid ascent and descent of Calvary Chapel/Dove Ministries. Both experienced a meteoric rise to prominence but were unable to maintain their respective reputations as worthy of national acclaim. Each was inspired by charismatic leadership, but neither had a solid foundation or adequate infrastructure. Both were predictable products of a Las Vegas culture that prized sudden success and instant gratification.

As late as 1986, all seemed to be going well with Dove International, but in reality there was trouble beneath the surface. Some of it stemmed from Walsh's innovative and non-traditional administration. The local newspaper and church leaders raised questions about his handling of church finances.[43] At best, there were poor bookkeeping records. At worst, there was misappropriation of funds. The problem was that there was no access to financial records to resolve the questions. Neither the congregation nor the governing board reviewed the church's financial records, hence there was no credible means to clear Walsh of the charges leveled against him.

By early 1986, Pastor John Michaels began plans for a church of his own. According to Walsh, Michaels began covertly soliciting potential members away from Dove Ministries. Unbeknownst to Walsh, Michaels had gained the endorsement of Chuck Smith, pastor of the mother church in Costa Mesa. The separation occurred in August 1986, when, according to Walsh, Michaels took approximately 600 members from the flock and started another Calvary Chapel in the Spring Valley area of Las Vegas. Michaels contested the 600 number, insisting that only about 150 came with him to begin the new church. Another Dove member, however, confirmed that the number was closer to 600, but that not all went with Michaels to start the new work. He believed many simply left Dove. They left because they were disgusted with Walsh's handling of the church split. Walsh publicly criticized Michaels and his followers for leaving Dove. Disgruntled parishioners took exception to Walsh using the Dove podium as a bully pulpit.[44]

43. Weier, "Scandal, Financial Woes Hurt Ministry," *Las Vegas Review Journal*, August 2, 1987.

44. Dennis Lee. Interview by author, November 2001.

Michael's departure was a personal blow to Walsh, and it had an initial impact upon Dove's growth and prosperity. Walsh claimed Dove's membership bounded back quickly and that its finances were not drastically affected. However, the mystique of Dove was shattered and the firewall of unity was penetrated. The irony was that Pat Walsh's ministry, populated largely by members solicited from other congregations, was itself victimized by a staff pastor courting members from Dove to begin his own congregation. With the formation of a second Calvary Chapel in Las Vegas, a tense rivalry developed between the two churches, manifested by personal conflict between Walsh and Michaels.[45] Walsh felt betrayed by Michaels. The former contended it was unethical for Michaels, who Walsh hired as an assistant, to openly recruit members from Dove. Michael's claimed he left Dove as a matter of principle. He no longer trusted Walsh and believed the integrity of the ministry had been hopelessly compromised. According to Michaels, Walsh's dictatorial leadership style and financial mismanagement sabotaged the ministry.[46]

In an effort to shore up the breech at Dove and secure more personal control over the church, Walsh exerted his authority as head of Dove International. John Perenti remained the official senior pastor, but Walsh retained ultimate control as something of an empowered godfather. As president of the corporation, he largely controlled the church's direction and retained firm control of the church's finances.[47]

In 1987, Dove Ministries began to collapse. The first cave-in was quite literal as a Dove maintenance worker fell through the roof and plunged to his death in January.[48] Another crisis emerged in February, when a young lady stepped forward and confessed to a leader of another charismatic church that she had been involved in an adulterous relationship with Pastor John Perenti.[49] When Walsh and the board of directors of Dove were apprised of the situation, they confronted Perenti and he

45. Pat Walsh. Interview by author, November 2000 and January 2001.

46. John Michaels. Interview by author, December 2001.

47. Duke Redburn. Interview by author, November 2001.

48. Anon., "Fall Kills Worker at Dove Ministries," *Las Vegas Sun*, January 29, 1987; Anon., "Dove Ministries Sued Over Wrongful Death," *Las Vegas Sun*, January 4, 1989.

49. Greg Massanari. Interview by author, April 2001. Rev. Massanari pastored another charismatic church in Las Vegas (Christian Life Community) during the 1980s. He was also a close personal acquaintance with several in leadership at Calvary Chapel/ Dove Ministries.

acknowledged the affair. He contended the relationship had ceased several months earlier and that his marriage was being restored. Because the relationship was terminated and Perenti confessed and vowed reform, a divided leadership of the church recommended that he be allowed to remain as pastor. He confessed his sin before the congregation, and they allowed him to continue as pastor.

When asked how the people could be so forgiving, one former board member explained that many of them had only recently converted and thus could readily understand how someone could make such a mistake. Besides, the member explained, the gospel was all about grace and forgiveness.[50] The congregation's theology of grace found expression in the case of Pastor John Perenti. Walsh used Scripture to defend his recommendation that the pastor be allowed to continue his ministry stating, "Was not King David also guilty of adultery? Yet he was not removed as king over Israel."[51] With David as an example, he defended his decision to stand behind Perenti who, himself, did not want to step down as pastor. One cannot be sure exactly what it was that motivated Walsh to recommend Perenti's retention. Former parishioners remember Perenti as an inspiring public speaker and believed Walsh feared losing his talented associate.[52] In any event, Walsh was determined to continue supporting Perenti, but the latter gradually became concerned about Walsh's financial accountability as well as the problems he himself inflicted on Dove Ministries. He resigned as pastor in September 1987. Walsh opposed Perenti's decision and pleaded in vain for the latter to reconsider. Walsh feared that another key pastor departing, perhaps to start another church in town, could further weaken Dove and worsen the huge financial burden incurred by the church.

More bad news broke later that year when local newspapers ran stories about the church's finances. The *Las Vegas Review Journal* accused Walsh of poor bookkeeping and draining of church funds for personal use. Questions were raised about church money used by Walsh in the purchase of a new house. There were also accusations that Walsh inappropriately invested church money in the stock market. Walsh insisted

50. Round Robin. Interview by author with several former members of Calvary Chapel/Dove Ministries, August 2000.

51. Pat Walsh. Interview by author, November 2000 and January 2001.

52. Round Robin. Interview by author with several former members of Calvary Chapel/Dove Ministries, August 2000.

that his only error was poor business judgment.[53] Other church members suspected something sinister was going on. The problem was no one could prove anything one way or the other, because Walsh had control of all the financial records and did not allow access to them. The publication of newspaper articles concerning Walsh's handling of finances moved the issue from an in-house topic to the public arena. The luster of Camelot was quickly tarnishing.

More unfavorable events continued to come to light. Milton "Duke" Duvall, another member of Walsh's pastoral team, came under a grand jury indictment for fraud.[54] Court papers charged that Duvall used false sales-pitches and high-pressure tactics to lure investors into a scam where Duvall utilized the funds for "excessive salaries and personal living expenses."[55] Civil authorities claimed Duvall netted more than $1.7 million in a scam couched in Scripture in which Duvall abused his power as a minister. Duvall eventually admitted his guilt and explained that his actions were triggered by "an excessive desire to win." The question comes to mind, *what* was he trying to win? He expressed remorse for hurting the very people he wanted to help.[56] Duvall was convicted and sent to prison for his white-collar crime. Shortly thereafter, another church leader, Tony Falcone, was convicted of a crime related to finances, and later went to jail for his part in a theft racket that operated in North Las Vegas. The ring stole televisions and sold them on the black market.[57] Throughout the controversy, the church remained solvent and still boasted a viable, albeit diminished, constituency. However, these negative revelations destroyed the image of innocence and the sense of moral and spiritual integrity that heretofore had defined the membership's self-perception.

The growing public scandal took its toll on Dove ministries. In addition to the all-too-public sins of Perenti, Duvall, and Falcone, allegations of child molestation were brought against two other Dove church youth ministry leaders.[58] These accusations never did result in convictions

53. Pat Walsh. Interview by author, November 2000 and January 2001.

54. Weier, "Pastors at Las Vegas Church Step Down," *Las Vegas Review Journal*, November 24, 1987.

55. Heider, "Ex-pastor of Dove Ministries Faces Trial," *Las Vegas Sun*, May 18, 1989.

56. LaVella, "Pastor Pleads Guilty to Fraud Charges in Dove Ministries Scandal," *Las Vegas Review Journal*, December 21, 1989.

57. John Michaels. Interview by author, December 2001.

58. Weier, "Pastors at Las Vegas Church Step Down," *Las Vegas Review Journal*, November 24, 1987.

because the minors involved would not testify, but further damage was done to the church's reputation and credibility. Financial support began dwindling, but the mortgage and other bills still had to be paid. People were murmuring and restless. One former elder told reporters that he "found corruption in God's house." He claimed to have been a board member for six years but was kicked out when he raised questions along with other board members.[59] As rumors circulated of financial misman-agement and doctoring of the church books, there was talk within the congregation of factions ready to leave and start other churches.

Local newspapers featured stories about the church's problems for several months. After Perenti's departure, Walsh was forced back into a more direct leadership at Dove. The church had accumulated a moun-tain of debt, the flock was much smaller, and the church's reputation was destroyed. Walsh's dream of Dove International planting churches across the country and around the world became a nightmare. The designa-tion "Dove" now conjured up so many negative associations that Walsh autocratically decided to change the name of the church again in 1988. This time the congregation came to be known as Hallelujah Fellowship. Rather than undertaking a critical examination of the church's infra-structure, Walsh simply used Satan as a convenient scapegoat. In vintage Pentecostal fashion, Walsh blamed the Devil for the church's tarnished reputation. By doing this, he was able to deflect criticism that otherwise would have been directed at him.[60] While problems continued to mount at Dove (Hallelujah Fellowship), Perenti laid low for a few months. He went out of active ministry and supported himself through secular employ-ment. Several months later, Perenti began conducting a Bible study out of his home. It is unclear whether or not he initially intended to develop this home study group into a full-fledged church, but in the end, that is what happened. On November 17, 1988, Meadows Fellowship began with Perenti as founding pastor. There were approximately one hundred twenty people present for the inaugural service.[61] Perenti learned many of the marketing techniques of his mentor, it is understood, and services were formatted in much the same fashion as Dove during its glory days.

59. Weier, "Scandal, Financial Woes Hurt Ministry," *Las Vegas Review Journal,* August 2, 1987.

60. Round Robin. Interview by author with several former members of Calvary Chapel/Dove Ministries, August 2000.

61. Ted Ramy. Interview by author, November 2001.

According to Walsh, Meadows was mothered (albeit reluctantly) by Dove Ministries.[62] By other accounts, Walsh was not at all pleased that another former associate started a new church which threatened to drain still more members from Hallelujah Fellowship.[63] One thing was clear at this point. Hallelujah Fellowship was in decline, and new churches like Calvary Chapel Spring Valley and Meadows Fellowship were on the rise.

Within a year, Meadows Fellowship drew up to seven hundred in weekly attendance. Perenti was more interested in business skills than spiritual credentials among his inner circle of leadership. He created an advisory board he dubbed his "pac" men. The official name was the Pastor's Advisory Council. They were not selected for their spiritual credentials but rather because they were good in business and marketing. Perenti held regular brainstorming sessions with them for ways to increase membership.[64] A young man named Ted Ramy supported Perenti in the establishment of Meadows. Ramy originally came to town to study Greek at Dove's River of Life Bible School, but he left Dove and joined Meadows when Perenti started the new church. Within a few months Ramy became Perenti's associate pastor and understudy. Together, they worked to give the congregation a stable base. Perenti had learned much from Walsh about building a congregation, and he confided a lot to his new assistant. Indeed, Perenti once made the revealing comment to Ramy about his pac men: "They are not spiritual leaders but they are good tithers."[65] Multitudes in attendance and finances seemed to be the core motivation and the definition of success for John Perenti.

Meadows Fellowship became the chic place for charismatic believers to attend church in Las Vegas. Potentially, a new Dove-like mega church was on the rise. Perenti was quickly regaining his popularity, and some prominent local citizens joined his church. Among them was an up-and-coming politician named John Ensign and tennis star Andre Agassi. Perenti took special interest in Agassi. The tennis star attended the church and invited Perenti to travel with him to tennis tournaments. It seemed Camelot was making a comeback, but then things fell apart once again.

62. Pat Walsh. Interview by author, November 2000 and January 2001.

63. Ted Ramy. Interview by author, November 2001.

64. Ibid.

65. Ibid.

One Sunday morning in November 1989, Perenti stunned the congregation with the announcement that he was resigning effective immediately. He informed his associate, Ted Ramy, of his intentions before morning worship and did not even return for the evening service. Perenti gave the reason for his decision was the need to spend more time with his family. Apparently, there were serious domestic problems, because within three weeks of his resignation, he filed for divorce. Perenti's days of pastoral ministry were over.[66]

Perenti designated Ramy to succeed him as pastor of Meadows Fellowship. It was not something Ramy saw coming, so he assumed the mantle in a state of shock. Walsh viewed the shake-up at Meadows as an opportunity to regain members of his congregation who defected to Meadows. He took out a large newspaper advertisement in the form of an open letter. It appeared in the religious section of the *Las Vegas Review Journal* and invited all former members of Dove (now renamed Hallelujah Fellowship) to return to the mother church.[67] Soon after, Walsh sent a leader from Hallelujah, a man named Mike Caldwell, to visit Pastor Ramy and demand that Meadows disband and return to Walsh's church. When Ramy refused to do so, Caldwell personally came into Ramy's office, pounded his fist on the desk and predicted that Meadows Fellowship would be destroyed. Ramy did not know whether to take the remarks as a threat or a dark prophecy. In any case, Meadows stood its ground and continued to operate as an independent church. A short time later, Caldwell had an affair with a woman at Hallelujah Fellowship, divorced his wife, and left the ministry. The legacy of Dove's defective leadership continued.

What remained of Dove Ministries was in shambles. The church was heavily in debt, and the crowd that only a short time before numbered in the thousands was now in the low to mid-hundreds. Splinter groups emerged. Several new churches began with some of them surviving and others folding after a short period. Some leaders left the area altogether and moved to other states where they started new ministries. Bob Coy, who was the youth pastor on staff, moved to Fort Lauderdale, and began another Calvary Chapel there. Kent Nottingham, who presided over Dove Ministries' schools, moved to Tallahassee, and began a ministry in

66. Ibid.

67. Anon., "An Open Letter to the Sheep at Meadows Fellowship . . ." *Las Vegas Review Journal*, November 18, 1989.

that city. In retrospect, Walsh put a positive spin on all the churches and ministries that came out of Dove. According to him, they were church plants that grew out of his vision.[68] However, not everyone agreed that the separations were so amicable. Those who left Walsh contended his interpretation was really an attempt to save face in the midst of a debacle.[69] Most of those who left the church did so without Walsh's blessing, but those members who left his church viewed the splits as "jailbreaks rather than the mother church giving birth to offspring."[70]

Walsh and Dove International had fallen victim to its own freelance style of ministry. On the positive side, its break with traditional churchianity breathed new life into spiritual seekers unable to relate to established denominationalism. However, on the negative side, a lack of ecclesiastical accountability and adequate infrastructure left it vulnerable to controversy, corruption and schism. Meanwhile, Walsh remained the titular head of Hallelujah Fellowship. Another pastor, Tim Bales, assumed Perenti's mantle of senior pastor, but Walsh remained president of Dove International.[71] Walsh continued to draw a salary even though he was not the official pastor. He also began lobbying for lifetime retirement support. This was done without the knowledge or approval of the congregation.[72] The fact that the church was already financially strapped did not deter Walsh from using the ministry to secure his own financial security. What began as a utopian dream of a diversified mega-church serving the Las Vegas Valley and expanding its influence across the nation and around the world, ended in all-too-public corruption and sexual escapades. Bitterness and fragmentation turned out to be the actual legacy. The departure of pastors and the creation of new congregations generated a sense of animosity and competitiveness. Many left completely disillusioned with Dove Ministries and harbored ill feelings towards Pat Walsh.

In studying the rise and fall of Calvary Chapel/Dove Ministries/Hallelujah Fellowship, there are a number of observations to be made regarding its initial success and sudden demise. The ministry rode the

68. Pat Walsh. Interview by author, November 2000 and January 2001.

69. Round Robin. Interview by author with several former members of Calvary Chapel/Dove Ministries, August 2000.

70. Ted Ramy. Interview by author, November 2001.

71. Weier, "Pastors at Las Vegas Church Step Down," *Las Vegas Review Journal*, November 24, 1987.

72. Duke Redburn. Interview by author, November 2001.

crest of a wave that carried Pentecostal Christianity throughout the 1970s and 1980s, the era of televangelism at its zenith. Jimmy Swaggart, the PTL Club, and the 700 Club were all popular television shows that mastered the art of mass marketing their brand of Christian faith. However, it was also the period in which the media exposed the flaws in national ministries and televangelists such as the Bakkers and Jimmy Swaggart were discredited. The blend of selective biblical literalism, experiential faith, charismatic personalities, and an entertaining presentation of the message were components in the making of a popular religious sub-culture. Pat Walsh understood the value of marketing his message in a way that would have popular appeal. The concert ministry featuring popular Christian artists, nationally known speakers, and timely films where all part of the mix that captured the attention of many who were interested in a new expression of Christianity. Walsh's ministry team was inexperienced, young, and largely self-educated. They were charismatic but too often valued style and delivery over content. Perhaps this was one of the factors that contributed to their personal failures. Lack of training and experience left them vulnerable to the pressures and temptations that often present themselves to those in the ministry. Sex, power, and money are allurements to which those in high profile places of leadership often succumb. These very issues were at the heart of Dove's demise.[73] The congregation was also too uncritical for its own good. Almost gullible in their acquiescence of all that went on, the lay leadership did not hold church ministries accountable. They became victims of the Pentecostal tendency to blindly follow charismatic leadership; believing their pastors have a special connection with the mind and heart of God.

In everything from staff appointments to financial records to name changes, laymen simply rubberstamped Walsh's desires. Perhaps disaster could have been averted if laypeople had dealt with issues before they became actual problems. Part of the naiveté of Walsh and the philosophy of ministry that governed Dove was a misunderstanding of sound principles of leadership. Although Walsh hid behind egalitarian rhetoric, in reality he was a leader who maintained his control over virtually every aspect of the church. The one place where no hierarchical structure existed was exactly where it was needed most. Walsh publicly ranked all pastors equal in status, but the fundamental human desire for power and

---

73. Dennis Lee. Interview by author, November 2001.

recognition created tension and rivalry in the formation of the leadership team. Ideally, the concept of multiple pastors all sharing the mantle of leadership sounded good, but in practice it set the stage for a power struggle. Walsh mistakenly believed he could assume a patriarchal role while his handpicked pastoral staff ran the church with unflinching loyalty. The desire for personal power outweighed a sense of submission to the founding pastor.

Even though Camelot crumbled due to lack of proper accountability, poor judgment, inexperience, and the timeless foibles of money, power, and sex, Dove Ministries made a lasting impact upon the Las Vegas Valley. Other churches borrowed elements of its style and marketing techniques, and the result was that their message became more appealing to the public. Disillusioned former members migrated to other churches in the valley all the wiser for lessons learned. Many joined churches with a denominational affiliation. They came to recognize the importance of infrastructure and accountability.

Pulitzer prize-winning author Charles Shepherd who wrote *Forgiven* (a definitive account of the rise and fall of the PTL television ministry), observed that part of what went wrong with the ministry of Jim and Tammy Bakker was that it grew too fast. He concluded that the rapid rise of their ministry, including fame, power, and money, caught them unprepared to responsibly handle it all.[74] This contributed to their misuse of finances and their unethical conduct. The Bakkers maintained they started out sincerely and honestly, but that money, celebrity status, and power came so fast they were unable to properly assimilate and responsibly handle the resources and opportunities that came with it. Laurence Moore, in *Selling God*, pointed out that the blurring of a distinction between spiritual and secular was both the genius and Achilles heel of Pentecostal televangelists. On the one hand, their carefully crafted message appealed to millions of Americans who embraced the new Pentecostalism. Unfortunately, employing the world's standards too often led to moral and ethical lapses that compromised the integrity of their ministries.[75] "Bakker wanted to be Walt Disney as well as Johnny Carson. His vision of a Christian theme park expanded into the multi-faceted complex of Heritage USA."[76]

74. Shepard Charles, *Forgiven*, 155–60.

75. Moore, *Selling God*, 3–4.

76. Ibid., 251.

Bakker told his followers they did not have to make the secular world their enemy, because it was theirs for the taking. Christians could enjoy the amenities and pleasures of popular culture. Bakker's world was a sort of reckless libertarianism.[77]

Much the same thing happened at Calvary Chapel Las Vegas. The church rose like a phoenix in the desert. Large crowds, a lot of money, and national exposure all coalesced to create a religious phenomenon the likes of which the valley never saw before. The church's leadership lacked the experience, training, and infrastructure to responsibly manage a mega-church. One former leader mentioned pride and independence as part of the recipe for disaster.[78] A group of self-taught, inexperienced, free-lance leaders took the church, in a short amount of time, from non-existence to Las Vegas' first mega church. They were not interested in the wisdom of seasoned pastors or the insight and safeguards provided by denominational oversight; hence, they became victims of their own arrogance and sense of superiority. About the same time Calvary Chapel/Dove was imploding, Jim and Tammy Bakker's televangelism empire was also self-destructing. A few years after the collapse of PTL a convicted, broken, and repentant Jim Bakker reflected on what went wrong with his ministry. While in prison one of Bakker's friends sent him a book written by Dietrich Bonhoeffer. Bonhoeffer was a German theologian/pastor during Hitler's reign of terror. He was eventually arrested and executed for resisting the Nazis. In a book entitled *Life Together*, Bonhoeffer wrote:

> Innumerable times a whole Christian community has broken down because it has sprung from a wish dream. The serious Christian, set down for the first time in a Christian community, is likely to bring with him a very definite idea of what Christian life together should be and to try to realize it. But God's grace speedily shatters such dreams . . . God will not permit us to live even for a brief time in a dream world. He does not abandon us to those rapturous experiences and lofty moods that come over us like a dream. God is not a God of the emotions but the God of truth . . . A community which cannot bear and cannot survive such a crisis, which insists upon keeping its illusion when it should be shattered, permanently loses in that moment the promise of Christian community. Sooner or later it will collapse . . . He who loves his dream of a community more than the Christian community itself

77. Ibid., 252.

78. Ted Ramy. Interview by author, November 2001.

becomes a destroyer of the latter, even though his personal intention may be ever so honest and earnest and sacrificial.[79]

Bonhoeffer's assessment and Bakker's own reflection on his undoing serves as a model to explain the troubles at Calvary Chapel/Dove Ministries/Hallelujah Fellowship in Las Vegas. The illusion of success became an end in itself. When the perpetuation of the illusion took the place of the priority of building a caring spiritual community, it set the stage for the dismantling of the congregation and the undoing of the ministry.

79. Bonhoeffer, *Life Together*, 26–29.

8

Patchwork Quilt

To borrow a term from Randall Balmer, Las Vegas Pentecostals constituted an ecclesiastical "patchwork quilt" with many diverse squares. A quilt represents folk-art; it requires the work of many hands and each contributor provides a personalized signature to the project.[1] Pentecostalism is not a monolithic movement but, like a patchwork quilt, is interconnected by diversity, cultural relevance, Biblicism, and passion. These are among the reasons for its expansion within different groups of people. It is one of the few major religious traditions that have historically offered a leadership role to women. From its inception women have served effectively as pastors, missionaries, and evangelists. Pentecostals utilized a resource that was relegated to support and secondary roles in most major denominations.

In this final chapter, a thumbnail sketch of various expressions of local Pentecostalism will be examined to provide a sampling of the diversity among Pentecostals in the Las Vegas Valley. Pentecostals are theological independents who construct formations of faith responsive to individual conscience and needs. Included here is a church that was pastored by an independent-minded woman. When she felt she did not fit any domination profile, she started one of her own. Another patch in the quilt was a minister who targeted his ministry to reach outsiders including prostitutes, motorcycle gang members, alcoholics, and drug addicts. Hispanics were still another patch. They tended to assimilate rather that segregate. The story of one such local Latino believer makes the point. On the other hand, Korean Pentecostals choose segregation over assimilation. This

---

1. Balmer, *Mine Eyes Have Seen the Glory*, 229.

Asian contingent made their faith nearly as much a community center as it was a spiritual fountain head. Let the quilting now begin.

ECHOES OF FAITH

Beale Elizabeth DeGroot was born in Jones, Oklahoma, in 1922. Her father died one month before her birth so her mother, Lizzie, raised her from infancy. Lizzy was a traveling evangelist; so the model for women in ministry was something with which Betrie grew up. DeGroot graduated from high school in 1940 and earned a business degree in 1941. While completing her formal education, she herself entered the ministry and held revival meetings in Oklahoma when she was just fifteen years old. In addition to the support of her mother, McCoy's childhood friend, Pearl Trumble, assisted in her ministry. Her relationship with Pearl Trumble was unusual. The two were lifelong friends and ministered together periodically during their younger years. After both were divorced, they became companions who lived and ministered together. Trumble spent many years in a supportive role as she labored alongside DeGroot in building the Echoes of Faith Ministries. In 1945, Ms. DeGroot founded an Assemblies of God church in Luther, Oklahoma. She married Frank McCoy of Luther Oklahoma in 1948. She enjoyed a happy marriage with Frank. He was employed as a county worker while McCoy continued her ministry, but he died just ten years later.[2]

McCoy was ordained as an Assemblies of God minister in 1949. She never received any formal theological training, but did earn a certificate through a non-accredited correspondence Bible school. McCoy was a proactive church planter and played a major role in the establishment of at least seven churches in Oklahoma. In 1957, she moved her ministry to California where she both started and salvaged churches. She moved back to Oklahoma in 1962 to assist her brother-in-law, Reverend George McCoy, but then responded to an invitation to help start a church in Wells, Nevada. For the rest of her career, Nevada would be her place of ministry.[3]

2. McCoy, *McCoy Autobiography*. An autobiographical paper.

3. Barbara Matza. Interview by author, November 2001. Mrs. Matza served as an assistant to McCoy at Echoes of Faith Ministries. After McCoy's retirement, Barbara and her husband assumed the pastorate of the church.

In 1970, McCoy married another minister, Reverend Delbert Price, and they pastored together in Henderson. McCoy's second marriage was short-lived and ended in divorce after only one year. The dissolution was something that bothered McCoy, because she did not believe it was biblically authorized. However, there were fundamental differences in the couple's understandings of the ministry. Her personal sense of calling and reliance upon the "Spirit's leading" prompted her to take exception to the Bible's literal teachings. There was, however, a price to pay for her decision, as she felt compelled to forfeit her credentials with the Assemblies of God denomination.[4] Additionally, there was more than just the divorce that motivated McCoy to separate from her denomination; she also felt her affiliation with the Assemblies was too confining.

Later that year, McCoy's mother joined her in Las Vegas and together they reopened a closed down church on Belmont Street in downtown Las Vegas.[5] In 1971, she established Powerhouse Ministry on 4th Street, where she developed an outreach which worked with kids on drugs, adult addicts, and prostitutes. McCoy always had great compassion for children and adults afflicted by vice and addiction.[6] These concerns became an effective driving force for her new ministry. McCoy insisted that it was not easy to be a woman in ministry, because other pastors from various denominations did not believe women should be in pastoral leadership. She encountered the most resistance from older members of the clergy; younger church leaders were more accepting of her. McCoy was a strict Biblicist, but she did not interpret the Bible like others did. She believed women had the same calling and potential to minister as did men. In her estimation, others read the Bible in the wrong way. She had the strength of conviction and persisted in ministry based on her own interpretation of Scripture.[7]

In 1973, McCoy organized Echoes of Faith. In 1975, McCoy's ministry moved to a permanent home on East Washington Street. She purchased an old building and started a coffee house ministry that later developed into a church she named Echoes of Faith. It was here that McCoy ministered until her retirement in 2001. The church was never

4. McCoy, Bertie. Interview by author, December 2001.

5. Barbara Matza. Interview by author, November 2001.

6. McCoy, *McCoy Autobiography*.

7. Ibid.

large in membership, but it was well known throughout the Las Vegas Christian community. She continued her emphasis upon ministry to the poor and homeless and also to female Strip workers. There were a number of showgirls that McCoy befriended and helped convert to Christianity. She is remembered for her generosity, because she often offered financial help to those in need even though she herself drove an old car and lived on a shoestring.[8]

There was also a missionary dimension to McCoy's ministry. She continued the planting of churches and was responsible for those established in North Las Vegas, Henderson, Tonopah, and Indian Springs. McCoy was no longer credentialed by a denomination, but that did not stop her from ministering, founding churches, and empowering others for ministry. Over the years, she ordained more than fifty individuals through the Echoes of Faith Corporation. Approximately half of those credentialed through her organization were women.[9]

Echoes of Faith was a small but multi-faceted ministry. The parish numbered between 150 and 200 people consisting of many seeking to overcome life-controlling problems and addictions. The church drew families who came from lower-middle-class to middle-class economic levels. The congregation was racially mixed with a consistent number of Hispanic members among the majority of white congregants. The church also sponsored feeding programs for the needy and established a Christian school that met in the church facilities.[10] McCoy had great hopes for the future of Echoes of Faith. She envisioned a sanctuary that would seat 2,500 people, a multi-purpose building that would accommodate school functions and social gatherings, and a six-story prayer tower that would also include a restaurant and bookstore. None of these dreams ever came true, but they demonstrated the kind of sanctified imagination and drive that defined Echoes of Faith and McCoy.[11]

It was McCoy who made Echoes of Faith quintessentially Pentecostal. As a strong woman driven by her own convictions, she was not about to subordinate her calling to any man. In typical Pentecostal fashion McCoy was confident that she could hear the voice of the Spirit herself. It did not

8. Barbara Matza. Interview by author, November 2001.

9. Ibid.

10. Ibid.

11. Echoes of Faith. *Homecoming Roundup, 18th Anniversary Celebration 1989*, 9.

matter what any denominational hierarchy taught; moreover, this woman was not restricted by a traditional literal interpretation of New Testament passages concerning the role of women in church and ministry. She relied on a pneumatic hermeneutic in hearing and applying the biblical message.

McCoy was an example of the opportunities that Pentecostalism afforded women. McCoy's strength of conviction and force of will were strong enough that she, in effect, started her own denomination when there was none that would accommodate her calling and ministry. It was not that she failed to command respect and acceptance by others, but she was determined to frame her ministry according to the convictions of her heart. Other ministers in town, in fact, respected her. She had to battle for their respect, but she eventually earned it through her accomplishments over the years.

GRAPEVINE FELLOWSHIP

Bud Higgenbotham moved to Henderson, Nevada, from Trona, California, in 1949. He came with a young family and a Bible school diploma earned at L.I.F.E. Bible College (the endorsed ministerial training institution of the International Church of the Foursquare). Bud supported his family as a gardener and carpenter while also starting a Bible study in his home. The Bible study group organized and developed a Foursquare church in Henderson. The parishioners were working class folk employed mostly at Hoover Dam, Nellis, and Basic Magnesium. Higgenbotham's initial stay in the valley was not long. After a year, he decided to move back to California. At the time, he did not know that the most fruitful years of his ministry would lead him back to the Las Vegas Valley.[12]

The Higgenbothams returned to Las Vegas in 1952. Bud came back to pastor the Las Vegas Foursquare Gospel Church, which had originally begun following a tent revival in August 1941. Reverend Ralph Barber was the founding pastor, and he and his wife served until 1952.[13] They left after the church fell on hard times. Higgenbotham, therefore, inherited a building with no people. His ministry started with only his family as a congregation. Not to be deterred, Higgenbotham planned a full order of

12. Teresa Miller. Interview by author, December 2001. Ms. Miller is the daughter of Pastor Bud Higgenbotham. She has been a member of her father's churches since moving to Las Vegas as a child.

13. *Pictorial Directory Calvary Church of the Foursquare Gospel*, 3.

service every Sunday even though only his family came. He reasoned that if he were not prepared for people to come, they never would. Finally, on Mother's Day 1952 the church had its first visitor, a woman without any children. Never one to be easily discouraged, Higgenbotham reasoned that the woman had a mother and it was therefore a good thing that she was present for his Mother's Day message. Eventually, others joined the congregation.

Bud and Agnes Higgenbotham ministered together at Las Vegas Foursquare Gospel Church for nineteen years and saw attendance increase to approximately 300 for Sunday worship. Under his leadership, the church purchased four and one-half acres of land on the corner of Cedar and 30th streets and built a new facility that was dedicated in May of 1968.[14] While leading the Las Vegas Foursquare Church, Higgenbotham crafted a traditional church that ministered primarily to families. The order of worship featured gospel songs, and the ministries and message of the church reflected conservative holiness theology. Higgenbotham was compassionate but adamant in his opposition to any contact with casinos and the world of gambling. Unlike Pat Walsh and others, he preached against the use of tobacco, alcohol, and worldly amusements such as theaters and dancing.[15]

In 1971, Higgenbotham felt his time at Foursquare Gospel Church was complete, so he resigned and moved to El Monte, California, to assume the pastorate of El Monte Foursquare Church where he and his wife served for approximately nine years. In 1980, he resigned and they moved back to Las Vegas to retire. Upon their return to the Las Vegas Valley, they joined the same church they founded some twenty years before. He began teaching a Bible study that specialized in ministering to recovering alcoholics. There was great interest in the study and it began to grow. After a while, the pastor of Neighborhood Church and Bud agreed that it would be a good idea to establish a new Foursquare church in the city.[16]

Thus, the idea was conceived that led to the creation of Grapevine Fellowship. The new congregation first met in 1979 at 2323 South Nellis Avenue. The nucleus of the new church consisted of a group of recovering alcoholics. Grapevine Fellowship began with a special emphasis

14. Ibid.

15. Agnes Higgenbotham. Interview by author, December 2001. Mrs. Higgenbotham was the wife of Pastor Bud Higgenbotham.

16. Ibid.

upon spiritual help for these people. Higgenbotham created a ministry that incorporated many elements of twelve step program of Alcoholics Anonymous, but added a distinctly Christian component. The higher power of Alcoholics Anonymous was reworked and personalized as faith in Jesus Christ.[17] He began with only twenty people. Bud Higgenbotham revamped his philosophy to meet the needs of a new congregation. While Las Vegas Foursquare had been a traditional holiness-minded Pentecostal church, Pastor Bud reformatted Grapevine for relevance to street people, many of whom battled addictions. Bud was always a traditionalist at heart, but the music, worship, method and message of Grapevine was modified to relate to the non-churched people that were his new target.[18]

This recipe for building a new faith community worked. Grapevine began to grow and by the early 1990s became a diverse congregation of almost 700 people. An interesting blend of individuals comprised the constituents. Traditional nuclear families made up one segment of the church's population. There were careful guidelines to ensure safety for the children because another portion of the congregation was composed of alcoholics, women with sexual addictions, promiscuous men, and drug addicts. There was yet another group within the congregation that existed in few churches. A number of bikers converted to Christianity and joined Grapevine. In fact, there were enough of them to form their own chapter of a national Christian motorcycle club called the "One Way Riders."[19]

Pastor Higgenbotham embraced all comers. He was especially interested in breaking through the color line that divided most other churches. He often made it a point to personally welcome people of color when they visited his church. As a result, Grapevine soon became an ethnically and racially diverse congregation. There were blacks, Hispanics, and Asians who worshiped with the white majority. Grapevine's ethnic diversity made it an exception among Pentecostal churches.

In his former ministry at Las Vegas Foursquare, Higgenbotham had looked askance at individuals claiming to be Christian who worked at questionable jobs in the casinos, but times had changed and so did he. At Grapevine, Pastor Higgenbotham took a pragmatic approach to applied theology. His open-mindedness and flexibility were consistent with

17. Higgenbotham, personal diary, entries from 1979 through 1981. Rev. Higgenbotham was the founding pastor of Grapevine Fellowship.

18. Teresa Miller. Interview by author, December 2001.

19. Ibid.

that of other Pentecostal leaders in the valley. Higgenbotham's church included a number of members who were dealers, bartenders, cocktail waitresses, and nightclub entertainers. Such professions were patently off limits to holiness-minded Pentecostals in other parts of the country. At one time, there was an associate pastor whose wife worked as a cocktail waitress. She asked Pastor Bud if she had to quit her job for her husband to hold his position in the church, and he said no. Her employment was a matter between her and the Lord.[20] Higgenbotham had not sold out his long-held standards, but he did refuse to impose them on individuals coming to the church with lifestyles that contradicted traditional Pentecostal values. Leaders were expected to toe the line and maintain lives that were above question or reproach, but newcomers were given the latitude to find their own way. Pastor Higginbotham believed the Holy Spirit would be the one to bring correction into peoples' lives. This was a departure from the legalism that was typical of Holy Spirit practitioners in other parts of the country.

Bud Higgenbotham's progressive approach caught the attention of others in his denomination. They were impressed with the innovative way he recast the gospel to reach people who typically did not feel accepted in Foursquare churches. L.I.F.E. Bible College in Los Angeles conferred upon him an honorary doctoral degree, and in April 1994 he was invited to speak before the Annual International Convention of the Church of the Foursquare Gospel. There were church leaders who traveled to Las Vegas to discover the secret of his success. His wife and daughter attributed his success to his openness and willingness to change. He was also remembered as a gracious and affectionate man who truly loved people and remained at the helm of Grapevine Foursquare church until his death in 1996.[21]

Bud Higgenbotham's ministry in Las Vegas illustrated the fluidity and pragmatism that has been a key to Pentecostalism's success. There were core convictions that guided his life, but he effectively distinguished between matters of first and secondary importance. He re-invented the formation of Pentecostalism to reach people who would otherwise never darken the doors of a church.

20. Ibid.
21. Ibid.

CRUZ OLAGUE

This patch of the quilt stitches in the story of one of the valley's most influential Hispanic Pentecostals. The story of Cruz Olague is significant because he personally embodied several characteristics of the Holy Spirit spirituality. Olague converted from traditional Catholicism to tongue-speaking Pentecostalism. His pilgrimage was consistent with the pattern of many other Latinos in that he integrated into predominately white Pentecostal churches. Upward mobility was another trait in the story of Olague, and he also represents the pattern of movement from a strong separatist brand of faith to involvement in an effort to transform culture.

Cruz Olague was born in 1934 into a Catholic Mexican family in Winslow, Arizona. His father Jessie, a professional prizefighter, died from injuries suffered in a boxing match when Cruz was just three months old. His mother was unable to raise Cruz alone, so he came under the guardianship of his grandparents. While growing up in Winslow, Cruz experienced the brunt of racial discrimination. As a Mexican, he could not swim at the public swimming pool because of a "whites only" rule.[22] As a young man, he joined the Navy at age eighteen and served in the Korean War.[23] After his discharge from the service, he married Thelma, a Hispanic woman from his hometown in Winslow.

It was in the 1950s that Cruz and Thelma moved their young family to southern Nevada. They settled in Henderson where Cruz worked in the grocery store business for several years while studying accounting at the University of Nevada.[24] It was during the late 1960s, while Cruz worked as assistant manager at Food Fair Market, that his religious conversion to Pentecostal faith took place. He was not spiritually fulfilled in the practice of the Catholic religion, because it seemed to him like mere ritualism.[25] During his quest for a more experientially-charged faith, a representative of the local chapter of the Full Gospel Businessmen's Association (a professional association of Pentecostal businessmen) gave Olague a copy of a popular evangelical book entitled *The Cross and the Switchblade*. This

22. Dorothy Olague. Interview by author, October 2002. Mrs. Olague was the wife of Cruz Olague.

23. Anon. "File for City Council," *Henderson Home News*, March 30, 1970.

24. Congressional Record, Proceedings and Debates of the 105th Congress, First Session, March 13, 1997, vol. 143, No. 32.

25. Dorothy Olague. Interview by author, October 2002.

book told of the conversion of a Latino New York city gangster named Nikky Cruz. Cruz attended the Full Gospel Business Men's Association meetings. His interest was piqued, and one night in his home, he made a personal profession of faith. This new brand of Christianity was more than creedal confession; it also included a "born again" experience. Shortly after his spiritual rebirth, Cruz received the Pentecostal experience of glossolalia. In the terminology of Pentecostalism, this was called the baptism in the Holy Spirit. Olague's new faith changed the course of his life.

Olague was a popular grocer, always friendly and outgoing towards the customers. He is remembered as a man with a soft spot in his heart for the poor.[26] He frequently donated groceries to needy families and took a personal interest in many of his customer's lives. Olague's popularity as the friendly grocer led some of his friends to urge him to run for Henderson City Council. Early in 1970, he declared his candidacy and ran on a platform that included lower water rates and releasing public lands for sale to individuals at affordable prices.[27] His campaign was a success, and he was elected to the city council serving the Fourth Ward. His election was noteworthy in that he received 53 percent of the vote on the primary ballot and thus did not have to face a second run-off election.[28]

Olague continued to work at the food store while serving on the Henderson City Council. During this period, he left the Catholic Church and began attending the Henderson Foursquare Church. This was a tongues-speaking congregation that was consistent with Olague's Pentecostal faith. Between 1971 and 1974, Olague's life included an interesting blend of business, politics, and religion. Among Olague's accomplishments was working with the Greenspuns in securing the purchase of public land for the development of Green Valley.[29] He was an active member of the Henderson City Council, speaking out on issues of land use and water management.[30] At the same time, he was a fervent practitioner of his Holy Spirit brand of Christianity. Olague believed very much

26. Anon., "Welcome Back," *Las Vegas Sun*, April 13, 1971.

27. Anon. "File for City Council," *Henderson Home News*, March 30, 1970.

28. Proclamation. By Governor Bob Miller of the state of Nevada, March 3, 1997.

29. Anon., "City, Hank Greenspun Arrive at Land Sale Agreement," *Henderson Home News*, November 16, 1971.

30. Reeves, "Huge Land Sale Looms for 'Little People,'" *Henderson Home News*, June 22, 1971.

in divine healing and would often take time while at work to pray for a needed miracle in the lives of his friends and customers. He claimed that sometimes oil would appear on the palms of his hands as he prayed for the sick.[31] As the local election of 1973 approached, Cruz Olague's uncle urged him to run for mayor of the city of Henderson. After counsel, thought, and prayer, Olague threw his hat in the ring and declared himself a candidate. He was a decided underdog as a Latino with only limited background in public service. His was a low budget campaign that concentrated on going door-to-door among the citizens of Henderson. To everyone's surprise, except Cruz's, he pulled off an upset victory and became the first Hispanic mayor in the history of Nevada.[32]

Olague's career continued to mix a blend of politics and religion. He was instrumental in purchasing land for a Pentecostal church in Henderson, and he used his political office to encourage the city council to approve a use permit.[33] During his administration, Olague led an effort to fight the consolidation of Henderson into Clark County.[34] He also sought to clean up city hall by instituting policies that kept public employees from taking advantage of their insider position in land purchases.[35] Olague's tenure as mayor was successful but short-lived. After less than two years in office, he resigned citing the need to spend more time with his family. Indeed, there probably were family problems, as Cruz soon thereafter divorced Thelma.

A change of venue seemed to be in order for Olague, so he moved within the Las Vegas city limits and began attending Trinity Temple Assembly of God Church. Wherever Cruz went, he continued to share his faith with those he met. It was during this time that he met Dorothy. This relationship revealed two characteristics of Cruz as a Hispanic Pentecostal. First, Dorothy was not a practicing Christian when she met Cruz. It was through his influence that she also converted to Pentecostal faith. Second, Dorothy was not a Latino. With Dorothy, Cruz developed

---

31. Dorothy Olague. Interview by author, October 2002.

32. Proclamation. By the Latin Chamber of Commerce, Las Vegas, NV, March 15, 1997.

33. Melvin Steward. Interview by author, October 1994 and January 2002. Rev. Steward pastored Trinity from 1974–84.

34. Anon., "Oppose Consolidation," *Las Vegas Sun*, November 5, 1973.

35. Anon., "Mayor Questioning Outside Activities of City Employees," *Henderson Home News*, October 4, 1973.

a relationship with and soon married a white woman. Olague was proud of his Mexican heritage, but integration rather than segregation was his philosophy. Besides a new wife, his career also changed, and he moved from the grocery business to employment in the convention business working for Greyhound Exposition.[36] Olague remained in the convention business and was an active member of Trinity Temple and later Calvary Community Assembly of God church.

In 1995, Olague was diagnosed with prostate cancer that had metastasized throughout his body. He was given only six months to live, but Olague believed in the power of prayer, and indeed, his cancer did go into remission. Olague testified that he had been healed. In 1998, he ran a spirited but unsuccessful campaign for mayor of Las Vegas. Shortly after this attempt to re-enter the political arena, he was diagnosed with leukemia and died in March of 2000.

As a testimony to the influence of Cruz Olague, there were several official citations in his honor. A tribute to Olague was entered into the United States Congressional Record at the 105th Congress in March of 1997. As Senator Harry Reid declared, "This prominent member of the Hispanic community has long believed that our racial and ethnic diversity is our nation's greatest strength. Cruz Olague spent his life tirelessly fighting on behalf of minorities, the elderly, and the poor. He has used his abilities for those who often lack a voice in our society. The work of this outstanding citizen has left a lasting impact on the lives of many Nevadans."[37]

In 1997, Henderson mayor Robert Groesbeck issued a proclamation honoring Cruz Olague's service and designated March 15th, 1997, as "Cruz Olague Day" in the city of Henderson.[38] Likewise, Governor Bob Miller designated the same day as "Cruz Olague Day" throughout the state of Nevada.[39] The Latin Chamber of Commerce of Las Vegas also issued a statement honoring the life and service of Cruz Olague.[40] Cruz Olague's life and faith reveals certain characteristics about Pentecostals.

36. Dorothy Olague. Interview by author, October 2002.

37. Congressional Record, Proceedings and Debates of the 105th Congress, First Session, March 13, 1997, vol. 143, No. 32.

38. Proclamation. By Mayor Robert Groesbeck of Henderson, NV, March 12, 1997.

39. Proclamation. By Governor Bob Miller of the State of Nevada, March 3, 1997.

40. Proclamation. By the Latin Chamber of Commerce, Las Vegas, NV, March 15, 1997.

Among Latinos, the Holy Spirit converts tended to assimilate rather than separate. This was true of Olague as well as many other Las Vegas Latino believers. This stood in contrast with African-Americans, Koreans and other ethnic groups that organized ethnic churches. Olague also provides an example of Pentecostals' upward mobility. In the early years, most "holy rollers" were from the underside of society but, like Cruz, through hard work, education, and an optimistic outlook, they moved into the cultural and economic mainstream. Finally, Olague represents this sub-culture's world view which changed during the course of the twentieth century.

In the early days, Pentecostals had little use for the historical, cultur-al, and political process. They believed human civilization was on a down-ward spiral to Armageddon. Hope was in their spiritual vocabulary, but it focused exclusively on the apocalyptic in-breaking of the kingdom of God. They lived in anticipation of the second coming of Christ. However, as the movement matured and many of the faithful moved into society's mainstream, their agenda changed. Cruz Olague embodied a new breed. He, like most other Spirit-filled believers, continued to live in anticipation of the Lord's return, but, at the same time, committed himself to the task of improving an existing world order.

FULL GOSPEL KOREAN

South Korea was one of the hotspots for growth of Christianity during the latter twentieth century.[41] The recasting of Korean spirituality consisted of a move from Buddhism to Christian faith. The world's largest Christian church was located in that country, and it was a Pentecostal congrega-tion affiliated with the Assemblies of God.[42] Reverend Paul Yonggi Cho, a converted Buddhist, was the pastor of Yoido Full Gospel Church in Seoul, South Korea.[43] It was a congregation that boasted a membership in excess of 900,000 by the year 2000.[44] Pentecostalism became so strong that the church began sending out missionaries to Africa, Russia, Japan, and the United States. The spread of Christian faith among Koreans was not just

41. Barrett, *World Christian Encyclopedia*, 624.

42. Vaughn, *The World's Twenty Largest Churches*, 35.

43. Burgess, et al.,. *Dictionary of Pentecostal and Charismatic Movements*, 102.

44. Barrett, *World Christian Encyclopedia*, 624.

confined to the home country, but also spread among Koreans living in other parts of the world.

Joel Kim was born in Japan in 1941. After World War II, as a six-year-old boy, he and his family moved back to South Korea. His parents were originally Buddhists but converted to Presbyterian Christianity. Joel accepted his parents' Christian faith and grew into adulthood as a nominal Presbyterian. Joel Kim received a good education in Korea and graduated with a bachelor's degree in music from Kyung Hee University. His intellectual capacity was further evidenced in that he spoke four languages fluently.[45]

In 1973, Joel Kim came to the United States with the intention of adopting it as his new permanent home. He opened a hamburger stand in Los Angeles in an effort to demonstrate full-time employment and obtain a green card. He did not like the hamburger business, and it lost money, but it was a means to the end of gaining permanent residence status. Joel's real passion was music. He was an accomplished pianist and also played the trumpet. Kim played at various nightclubs in the evenings after the hamburger stand closed. By the mid-1970's he was married with children. His dream was to become financially established and get a full-time job in the entertainment business. Kim, however, was a heavy drinker and smoked four packs of cigarettes a day. He often tried to break these habits, but could not do so. A spiritual breakthrough occurred in 1977 when his wife, Sook Ja, was reading her Bible. She had been afflicted with a lung and kidney disease, and one day while reading Scripture, she felt a physical sensation throughout her body. She believed she had been healed. After she went to the doctor, who confirmed her belief, Joel was deeply impressed by his wife's experience. One night he claimed he heard a voice that he interpreted to be from God. The voice directed him to turn in the Bible to Romans 12:21. The verse read: "Do not be overcome by evil, but overcome evil with good." He immediately prayed and asked the Lord to deliver him from smoking and drinking. He maintained he was instantly delivered and lost all desire for his heretofore controlling habits.

Kim left the Presbyterian denomination and began attending a Pentecostal church in Los Angeles. The years 1977–79 were Kim's formative years. His spiritual leaders encouraged him to begin pursuing theological studies so he enrolled at Bethesda Bible College in Los Angeles.

45. Joel Kim. Interview by author, December 2001. Rev. Kim was the founding pastor of Full Gospel Las Vegas Church.

Soon thereafter, he received the Pentecostal experience of speaking in other tongues. In 1980, church leaders recognized leadership potential in Kim and began talking to him about heading up a Bible study for Koreans in Las Vegas. There were about nine Korean residents in Las Vegas who had formerly been members of the huge Pentecostal church in Seoul, South Korea. They were eager to begin a church in Las Vegas that would reach the growing local Korean population. For a year and a half, Kim agreed to travel to the city on weekends to lead the small Bible study group. Under his leadership, the ministry flourished and he soon organized as a church. The burgeoning congregation soon needed to find more space.

The new church affiliated with the Assemblies of God, and Pastor Kim approached Pastor Mel Steward about borrowing Trinity Temple's facilities. Pastor Steward agreed to this arrangement.[46] The Korean church continued to expand. New members included international students studying at local colleges, spouses of military personnel stationed at Nellis Air Force Base, and workers employed at local hotels and casinos. Among the early converts who joined the church were singers known as the Kim Brothers and Kim Sisters (no relation to Joel Kim). They were nationally known performers who played on TV and at various local hotels and nightclubs. Pastor Kim maintained that most of the church's growth was the result of new conversions with a large percentage of new members who converted from Buddhism.[47]

By 1982, the church again was experiencing growing pains. Both Trinity Temple and Full Gospel were growing congregations with very active programs, and the two churches began feeling it was time to part company. Full Gospel needed a full-time facility that would accommodate the needs of a rapidly growing congregation.[48] Kim relocated the congregation to a Greek Orthodox Church facility on Bledsoe Avenue near Nellis Air Force Base. The building had been for sale since the Orthodox congregation quit using the facility, so Full Gospel decided to buy it. Finally, Full Gospel Korean Church had a permanent home. The church continued to grow, and its ministries broadened and expanded.

46. Melvin Steward. Interview by author, October 1994 and January 2002.
47. Joel Kim. Interview by author, December 2001.
48. Ibid.

Full Gospel's first priority was to be an evangelistic center. Its primary mission was to bring people to a confessing faith in Christ. One of the means Kim employed to attract new members was the creation of home Bible studies. By this means, he spread the Gospel and built fraternal spiritual relationships among members of the congregation. Another means of outreach was assisting Korean newcomers to the city. The church helped them by locating housing, providing financial assistance, and finding jobs. Full Gospel achieved its goal of becoming an aggressive missionary church. Following the pattern established by Full Gospel in Seoul, Korea, the Las Vegas church built seven other churches in the Philippines, China, Russia, Africa, and South America. Pastor Kim led the charge in planting new churches by traveling to foreign countries to preach and help organize a nucleus that would serve as the foundation for new congregations.[49] As a result, this local church became an international church in a very short time.

By the early 1990s, Full Gospel claimed an active membership of over 1,000 people.[50] Pastor Kim's aggressive leadership style, coupled with a growing Korean population and the continuing Korean interest in Christianity, all coalesced in the establishment of a large ethnic Korean Assemblies of God. Kim's success in creating a thriving church was, in part, the result of his ability to frame his message in a manner that met the immediate needs of the people he was trying to reach. He knew who they were and adapted his methods and message to achieve his goal. Many came to town and found employment in some aspect of the entertainment industry. However, the Koreans tended to stay away from more controversial jobs, such as erotic dancing, bartending, or dealing. Kim did not preach against gaming-related vocations preferring to leave such choices to individual members. In his view, such decisions were best made under the personal guidance of the Holy Spirit. A number of his congregants went into business for themselves, and Kim did everything in his power to support and encourage their enterprises. Once a year, he personally visited his church members' business establishments. Kim prayed with them asking specifically for God's blessing on their businesses.[51]

By the late 1980s, Full Gospel Korean Assembly of God emerged as the single largest Korean community organization in Nevada. Since

49. Ibid.
50. Ibid.
51. Ibid.

Las Vegas had no Korean neighborhood like Los Angeles, the founders also designed this church to serve as a cultural center for Korean community life in Las Vegas. In 1983, Pastor Kim organized an annual community event for the benefit of the local Koreans. In August of each year the church rented Artimus Ham Hall on the campus of the University of Nevada Las Vegas for the annual gathering that featured food, drama, and concerts. It consistently drew more than one thousand people in attendance, many of whom were not members of Full Gospel. The impact of Full Gospel upon the local Korean community drew the attention of state politicians. Among those who spoke at Full Gospel Church were Governor Richard Bryan and Senator Harry Reid.

In many ways, Full Gospel Korean Assembly of God fit the profile of ethnic churches described by H. Richard Niebuhr in The Social Sources of Denominationalism.[52] It became a port of entry into American culture for Koreans who moved to the Las Vegas Valley. Elements of their native culture were retained, and it was a friendly community where their mother tongue was still spoken. The church also served to help assimilate Koreans into the American work force. There was help extended to newcomers in finding jobs and housing in their new country.

The preceding sketches of local churches were consistent with the image of a patchwork quilt. Whites, blacks, Hispanics, Koreans, and other ethnic groups were all part of the quilt as were both men and women. They were politically, socially, theologically, and economically diverse. Still, they held certain things in common, including the Lordship of Christ, the authority of Scripture, a born again experience, the present day ministry of the Holy Spirit, and the expectation of the second coming of Christ. While holiness codes varied from church to church, another common characteristic was their pragmatism. Las Vegas Pentecostals were consistent with the national and international pattern of fashioning their message to fit a given context.

---

52. Niebuhr, *The Social Sources of Denominationalism*, 200–233.

9

Conclusion

THE LAS VEGAS AREA has historically been home to myriad religious communities. The city has never been the spiritual wasteland of popular perception. Religion was an integral component of southern Nevada's native Paiute civilization and has been at the heart of the white man's settlement of this desert region. Brigham Young's vision for Deseret prompted the first American pioneers to build a Mormon fort in what later became Las Vegas. When town building began in earnest in 1905, the Methodists, Episcopalians, and Catholics were at the heart of the effort. These churches strengthened the basic values necessary to establish and then maintain civility in this fledgling frontier community.

When the entertainment industry became the backbone of the local economy, it only enhanced the need for religious leaders and institutions to sustain the effort of maintaining a spiritual presence in Las Vegas. Gambling predictably attracted many unscrupulous individuals, so the need was magnified for honest and reliable people to work in the hotels and casinos. Howard Hughes certainly recognized the value of religious people to keep his empire afloat. Hughes hired Mormons and placed them in strategic positions in his corporation, because he believed that their religious convictions made them trustworthy.[1] Paul Lowden, owner of the Hacienda and Sahara hotels, was another example of a high profile employer who hired born-again Christians. He, like Hughes, recognized that employees with religious values were dependable and productive employees. Even Ted Binion, though not a religious man, donated money to build a church at the behest of some of his spirit-filled employees.

1. Bradley, "Las Vegas and the Mormons," BBC video aired 05/01/00.

Las Vegas' population grew throughout the twentieth century. Churches in general increased in size and number as more and more people called Las Vegas home, and Pentecostalism, in particular, was one of the city's fastest-growing religious groups. People came to the valley to make a fresh start in the pursuit of better lives. Las Vegas provided good jobs, affordable housing, and a frontier spirit that welcomed new ideas and industry. Many newcomers joined local churches because they viewed religion as part of the recipe for a successful and responsible life. Local churches also attracted new adherents who were damaged by addictions to gambling and alcohol. The religious community helped reassemble their broken lives. Families were interested in churches because parents desired that their children be nurtured in traditional values.

They wanted to base their families and friends on an infrastructure of honor, integrity, and proven American virtues. The churches were the beneficiaries of this quest.

Pentecostalism quickly and deeply engrained itself as an important part of the local spiritual environment. While Las Vegas Pentecostals were prolific, they were not monolithic. They were ethnically, socially, professionally, and economically diverse. The enthusiast configuration of faith began here as a working class movement in the 1930s with working class people populating Spirit-filled churches.

The emergence of local Pentecostalism mirrored the pattern of American revivalism in that it was strongly experiential. America's spiritual awakenings were historically characterized by a religion one could "feel." This stood in stark contrast to the Protestant Reformation that emanated from universities or from the English Reformation that was initiated by the ruling monarch Henry VIII. Common people fueled American revivals. This was true of the First Great Awakening led by George Whitfield, the Second Great Awakening ignited by a non-seminary trained lawyer named Charles Finney, and the Third Great Awakening led by a former shoe salesman named D. L. Moody. The founders of Las Vegas Pentecostalism were working class people, including such ordinary people as an African-American couple known as Dad and Mother Russell, an itinerate preacher named C. C. Cox, an obscure Hispanic pastor remembered as Brother Francisco Moreno, and women like Emma Jacobsen and Lola Hayes. All of these individuals were vital to the establishment of Pentecostalism in Las Vegas as were the blue-collar white laborers and southern African-American migrants who comprised the majority of worshippers in the first local Pentecostal churches. In this respect, they resembled first- generation Pentecostals elsewhere the nation. Vincent Synon, Robert Anderson, Harvey Cox, and Grant Wacker all noted the grass-roots origin of these pneumatic believers.

Las Vegas Pentecostalism may have begun among lower middle-class working class folk, but it did not stay there. As the movement grew, many members moved up the social and economic ladder. There were several factors that contributed to the Pentecostals' economic development and improved social standing. The entire black community benefited from new employment opportunities when job discrimination in the hotels and casinos ended in the 1970s. This change in the job market enabled many to obtain higher paying positions and social status. Black Pentecostals re-worked their holiness codes to take advantage of new economic opportunities.

White Pentecostal churches gained social acceptance as more affluent and better educated segments of the population began frequenting their churches. While there was still a large number working in lower middle class occupations, many second-generation Pentecostals and new converts came from the solidly middle and upper middle class strata of society. Their work ethic, religious values, and determination to educate their children created a Pentecostal subculture conducive to financial success. Local Pentecostals exemplified the pattern recognized by Niebuhr. In his book, The Social Sources of Denominationalism, he noted the tendency of churches serving the underclass to become congregations of the middle class once these churches assimilated into mainstream American society.[2] This process was clearly evident in the evolution of Trinity Temple and the rapid rise of the original Calvary Chapel Las Vegas. In the 1970s and 1980s, Trinity changed from an exclusively poor working class congregation to a large, diverse fellowship that included local politicians, entertainers, white-collar professionals, as well as blue-collar workers. Calvary Chapel/Dove Ministries skipped the underclass phase altogether. From its inception, this church attracted young, middle class adults infatuated with the anti-establishment mentality of the times.

Zion Rest Mission and the Westside Church began as integrated churches, as whites, blacks, and Hispanics worshipped side by side. Just alike the Azusa Street revival of 1906, ethnicity was not a barrier. In

---

2. Niebuhr, *The Social Sources of Denominationalism*, 27–28.

time, however, that changed as the inter-racial characteristic of the local Pentecostal churches became the exception rather than the rule. Sunday worship became a segregated hour as people joined churches that shared a racial affinity.

Color was one reason for the move away from integrated churches, but that does fully explain the drift apart. Interviews with black Pentecostals who were here since the 1950s revealed that most African-Americans preferred worshipping in black churches. There were various reasons for this. Pentecostals with southern roots comprised a large percentage of Westside congregations. Their church affiliation helped create a sense of community with others who came from the same region of the country. Another reason was differing worship styles. African-Americans went to church more often than whites, their services were longer, and their music was more energized. A number of African-American congregants said they visited Anglo churches from time to time but felt more at home in their Westside black Pentecostal fellowships. The separatism was so complete that one black pastor noted he did not even realize there were white Pentecostal churches in the valley until after he had been here for several years.[3]

Pentecostalism is a culturally adaptable expression of Christianity. Grant Wacker put it this way: "One is struck by how deeply American the Pentecostal movement was, first in its primitivist certitude, and second and perhaps more important in its pragmatic effectiveness."[4] It has the flexibility to recast itself to fit a given sub-culture. This was one of the reasons for its dramatic success in such distinctive cultural settings as southern California and Las Vegas.

A decision to revise the message to fit Las Vegas was not unanimous. Emma Jacobsen was wary about the changes that transformed Trinity Temple into one of the largest congregations in the city. She preferred the old ways and only reluctantly went along with many of the new ideas. Lola Hayes, who founded Christ Holy Sanctified Church, was even more strident in her opposition to rethinking the established holiness codes. She refused to adapt her message to contemporary time and culture.

---

3. Hall, Carruth. Interview by author, February 2000. Bishop Hall has been active in the Church of God in Christ since the early 1950s. He served as pastor of Greater St. Paul Church of God in Christ, and since 1993 has been bishop over the state of Nevada.

4. Wacker, *Heaven Below*, 197–216.

Perhaps this was one of the reasons her church never approached the size of other Pentecostal churches that were more open to change.

Pentecostalism was born out of the holiness tradition. Holiness Christians emphasized a prescribed code of acceptable Christian behavior that excluded drinking, dancing, movies, tobacco, alcohol, sex outside of marriage, and gambling. This brand of Christianity had little in common with the potential vices of Sin City. The earliest local Pentecostals maintained a separatist stance against the questionable elements of the culture, but with the passage of time, assimilation, and converts who came from the entertainment industry, local Pentecostals adapted their message to better fit the realities of life in the Las Vegas Valley. Chapter 6 underscored the culturally flexible dimension of Pentecostalism. If the church had not recast its message to allow for the inclusion of new converts coming in from the Strip, it would not have attracted literally thousands of people who joined Pentecostal and charismatic churches while keeping their jobs as dealers, dancers, gamblers, and the like.

The principle of pragmatism held true in the black Pentecostal churches as well. Their inherited holiness codes forbade involvement in "worldly" behavior, but when one's ability to earn a living was at stake, exceptions were made whether it be working in a casino or driving a beer truck. The traditional concept of separation from the world was reinterpreted when a black choir received an invitation to perform on the secular stage. An opportunity to sing at a local hotel called for reconsideration of a long standing separatist theology. African-American Pentecostals did not formally condone participation in the entertainment industry, but they rationalized their acceptance of jobs in the Las Vegas "sin culture" as an opportunity to spread the gospel among people who would never darken the door of a church.[5]

The contextual dimension of Pentecosalist holiness codes was further evidenced in the success of Calvary Chapel/Dove Ministries. This church was a testimony to the success of a pragmatic marketing strategy. For all his shortcomings, Pat Walsh had a knack for effectively marketing religion in Las Vegas. He understood how to frame the Christian message to appeal to the counter-culture generation. The music, dress, and message were all carefully crafted to appeal to the emerging baby

5. Hall, Carruth. Interview by author, February 2000. Bishop Hall has been active in the Church of God in Christ since the early 1950s. He served as pastor of Greater St. Paul Church of God in Christ, and since 1993 has been bishop over the state of Nevada.

boomers. The capacity to redesign the outward trappings of Christian faith and practice were important elements in the Las Vegas Pentecostal churches that grew in influence and numbers. Pentecostals were more concerned about existential relevance than established formality.

Whether it was C. C. Cox's linkage between the church and the community, Bill Sharpe's show-time rendition of the faith, Mel Steward's openness to converts coming from off the Strip, Bud Higgenbotham reaching out to drug addicts and bikers, Pat Walsh appealing to counter-culture oriented young adults, or Joel Kim forging a spiritual/cultural foundation for the city's Korean population, these local Pentecostal leaders all had the remarkable capacity to tailor their version of Pentecostalism to target a specific audience. Praxis triumphed over tradition and relevance over ritual.

The independent, creative spirit of Las Vegas Pentecostals was clearly part of the recipe for success, but the lack of regard for institutional authority, and a willingness to readily abandon the old ways in an attempt to appeal to popular mainstream culture, sometimes came at a high cost. For example, Pentecostalism in Las Vegas certainly had its share of questionable leaders. The independent, free-lancing ways of Pastor Bill Sharp of Trinity Temple and several members of the pastoral staff at Calvary Chapel/Dove Ministries led to their demise. They became a law unto themselves and, in the end, sabotaged the very ministries their savvy and creativity initially caused to flourish.

Some disgraced Pentecostal ministers may have been charlatans who deliberately exploited a situation, but in other instances, leaders simply may not have been properly prepared for the rigors of pastoral ministry. Few local Pentecostal pastors possessed a formal theological education. Most were self- taught ministers who relied on personal charisma and marketing acumen. For a season some of these self-educated clergymen enjoyed the limelight, but a lack of infrastructure and meaningful accountability left them vulnerable to their own foibles. In a sense, they were victims of their own determination to take shortcuts. The attention and acclaim they attracted proved more than they could handle. Without an adequate system of checks and balances there was little to curb their excesses until the damage had already taken place.

The trademark doctrine of historical Pentecostals was their distinctive understanding of the Holy Spirit. For the early twentieth century founders of the movement, the manifest presence of God was considered to be an experiential phenomenon. Authentic faith was more than creedal confession or denominational affiliation. A personal experience of the Holy Spirit was the litmus test for effectual Christianity. Las Vegas Pentecostalism witnessed both the positive and negative implications of "Spirit-led" faith. An Important dimension of their understanding of the Holy Spirit was the Spirit's role in the proper interpretation of Scripture. This dynamic relationship between Word and Spirit provided a firm footing with a flexible application of the Christian message. It was this pneumatic hermeneutic that distinguished Pentecostals from fundamentalists.

In a positive light, most local leaders utilized their freedom in the Spirit to craft fresh formations of faith that related to the unusual cultural setting of Las Vegas. In a post-modern culture devoid of external absolutes, the absolute of the Holy Spirit provided the foundation that legitimized fresh expressions of applied Christian living. Their understanding of the manifest presence of God became their foundation for life.

However, in the experience of other local Pentecostal leaders, their "Spirit" theology proved to be a problem. In the absence of a strong denominational accountability and without seasoned educated clergy, several Pentecostal leaders justified controversial actions as the "leading of the Holy Spirit." The dilemma was: how could one distinguish the Spirit's leading from what sometimes turned out to be nothing more than a cover justifying poor judgment or self-indulgence? An undiscerning congregation often went along with the desires of the charismatic leader believing him to be led by the Spirit. It was not until after damage was done that they realized the gravity of errors in judgment.

A peculiar blend of democratized Christianity and authoritarianism characterized a number of churches in this study. This was true of Trinity Temple, The Upper Room Church of God in Christ, and Calvary Chapel/Dove Ministries. Bill Sharp, C. C. Cox, and Pat Walsh all exerted a mesmerizing influence over their flocks. Their loyal followers believed there was a special anointing resting upon the pastor, and the ministers themselves often believed this was true. The agendas, priorities, and messages of the leaders were to be followed unquestioningly by the congregation. When a member of the congregation questioned a pastoral decision, it was often viewed as an act of insubordination. These pastors tolerated no questions when numerical growth, conversions, and dynamic worship services were occurring with regularity.

In the aftermath of certain leaders' indiscretions, gullible parishioners learned from their mistakes in the past. One of the insights gained was the danger of unchecked, charismatic leadership vested in a single personality. The democratic dimension was evident in the fact that the life of the church was configured to have a popular appeal. The songs, messages, the ministries, and presentations all reflected the needs, desires, and tastes of the people the leaders sought to reach. Local church leaders modified ground rules for inclusion, and embraced individuals who did not fit the mold of holiness-minded church members in other settings. If the churches were to grow and remain financially solvent, they had to be inclusive and careful not to alienate those upon whom they depended for support.

Christians have long sought a greater ecumenism. Division between Protestant and Catholic and the bewildering array of clandestine denominations rendered Christianity a splintered world religion. The National Council of Churches and the World Council of Churches were organizational attempts to forge unity amidst the diversity. However, the results of these efforts were meager at best. Twentieth century Pentecostalism accomplished a greater ecumenism than any of the ecclesiastical efforts of mainstream denominations. Pentecostals emphasized a unity based on a shared experience with the Holy Spirit. This formula attracted constituents from virtually every denominational background. C. C. Cox's Church of God in Christ included members from Baptist and Methodist background, and the predominately white Pentecostal churches boasted congregations consisting of Catholics and Protestants from virtually every expression of faith. They held in common a spirituality that was deemed more important than loyalty to a denominational heritage.

An ancient biblical proverb reads "As iron sharpens iron so one man sharpens another" (Proverbs 27:17). This verse found expression in Las Vegas. One might think the encounter between the church and the Strip would, like oil and water, be mutually exclusive, but such was not the case. The two communities actually co-existed in a paradoxical relationship. The Strip opened a new stage for churches to present the gospel in a culturally relevant manner by motivating Pentecostals to rethink their concepts of grace, piety and morality, and to overcome petty legalism. It also provided a steady flow of potential new believers as people hurt by the city's vices sought spiritual help. Holiness- minded Pentecostals provided the casinos and hotels with quality employees who were defined by a good work ethic, traditional values, and wholesome character. They also opened the door of faith to people considered by many traditionalists to be reprobate outcasts. The churches provided roots, a sense of family, a moral compass, and spiritual nourishment. It was a genuine oasis in an environment often deceived by mirages.

Perhaps the dynamic relationship between Pentecostal faith and the Las Vegas Strip is more of a glimpse of things to come than an exception to the rule. It has been argued that this resort city is the leading edge of what is becoming Main Street America. If this is so, then Pentecostalism likewise is rising as a mainstream spirituality. In an effort to interpret emerging trends, the Las Vegas experience may well represent a national portend of things to come.

In a very real way the church and the Strip have sharpened each other. The Apostle Paul once wrote words that aptly describe the reality of a thriving Pentecostal faith in the entertainment capital of the world, "Where sin abounded, grace did much more abound" (Romans 5:20).

Bibliography

PRIMARY SOURCES

Interviews

Abbey, Colleen. Interview by author, April 1992. Mrs. Abbey became a member of Trinity in the early 1960s. She was active in various ministries of the church and served as Women's Ministries director in 1990.

Arnold, Brenda. Interview by author, April 1992. Mrs. Arnold attended Westside Church (later Trinity Temple) in 1940.

Bennett, Marian. Interview by author, February 1996. Rev. Bennett has been pastor of Zion Methodist since 1960.

Cottingham, Dawn. Interview by author, November 1994. Ms. Cottingham was a dancer who performed with various Las Vegas strip shows in the late 1970s.

Cox, Ethel. Interview by author, October 2000. Mrs. Cox was a long-time member of the Cox's Upper Room Church of God in Christ. She was also sister-in-law to Bishop C. C. Cox.

Davis, Willie. Interview by author, February 1996. Pastor Davis has pastored Second Baptist Church since 1978.

DeVilbiss, Mary. Interview by author, October 1994. Mrs. DeVilbiss was the wife of Bob DeVilbiss. He held a Bible study on the Las Vegas strip from 1972–78 and was the Bible Answer Man on KILA Christian radio in Las Vegas from 1971–78.

French, Jack. Interview by author, March 1992. Mr. French is owner and manager of KILA Christian radio station established in Las Vegas in 1972.

Grauberger, Eldon. Interview by author, September and October 1994. Personal diary, January 1974. Mr. Grauberger served as a board member of Trinity during Bill Sharp's pastorate.

Hall, Carruth. Interview by author, February 2000. Bishop Hall has been active in the Church of God in Christ since the early 1950s. He has served as pastor of Greater Saint Paul Church of God in Christ since 1964 and has been bishop over the State of Nevada since 1993.

Harris, Francis. Interview by author, August and September 2000. Mrs. Harris has lived in Las Vegas since 1942. Her husband was pastor of Prayer Church of God in Christ from 1961–70.

Higgenbotham, Agnes. Interview by author, December 2001. Mrs. Higgenbotham was the wife of Pastor Bud Higgenbotham.

Hoggard, David. Interview by author, February 1996. Mr. Haggard was a leader in the black community. He served as head of the local chapter of the NAACP from 1955–

59 and was director of the Equal Opportunity Board from 1965–82. He was also an active member of Zion Methodist Church.

Ishmael, Herman. Interview by author, December 2001. Bishop Ishmael has been a member of Christ Holy Sanctified Church since 1952. He served as pastor from 1976–2000.

Jones, Ken and Jenny. Interview by author, October 1994. Mrs. Jones was a dancer on the Las Vegas Strip during the 1970s.

Kim, Joel. Interview by author, December 2001. Rev. Kim was the founding pastor of Full Gospel Las Vegas Church.

Lee, Dennis. Interview by author, November 2001. Rev. Lee was a member of Calvary Chapel since the early 1980s and eventually pastored Hallelujah Fellowship.

Martin, Betty. Interview by author, October 2000. Fictitious name used by the interviewee at her request since she was still a prominent member of Westside Church and the community.

Massanari, Greg. Interview by author, October 1994 and April 2001. Rev. Massanari pastured another charismatic church in Las Vegas (Christian Life Community during the 1980s). He was also a close personal acquaintance with several in leadership at Calvary Chapel/Dove Ministries.

Matza, Barbara. Interview by author, November 2001. Mrs. Matza served as an assistant to McCoy at Echoes of Faith Ministries. After McCoy's retirement, Barbara and her husband assumed the pastorate of the church.

McAuliffe Kevin. Interview by author, January 2000. Rev. McAuliffe has pastored Saint Elizabeth Ann Seton Church in Summerlin, Nevada, since July 1, 1997.

McDonald, Denise. Interview by author, November 1994. Ms. McDonald was an ice skater in various Las Vegas shows during the late 1970s.

Michaels, John. Interview by author, December 2001. Rev. Michaels was an associate pastorwith Pat Walsh from 1982–86 at Calvary Chapel/Dove Ministries. He left Dove Ministries to start a second Calvary Chapel work in Las Vegas.

Miller, Louise. Interview by author, September 2000 and October 2001. Ms. Miller moved to Las Vegas as a young girl in 1943. She has been a member of Cox's Upper Room/ Pentecostal Temple since that time. She has served in numerous leadership capacities in the church including Sunday School teacher, president of the youth group, usher, choir member, and head of the Deaconess Board.

Miller, Teresa. Interview by author, December 2001. Ms. Miller's father, Bud Higgenbotham, pastored the Las Vegas Four Square Church from 1951–70. She has been a member of her father's churches since moving to Las Vegas as a child.

Nighswonger, Ellenore. Interview by author, October 1992. Mrs. Nighswonger became a member of Trinity in 1931. She is the daughter of Emma Jacobson.

Morgan, Lupe. Interview by author, October 2002. Mrs. Morgan is the daughter of Albert and Jessie Rodriguez.

Olague, Dorothy. Interview by author, October 2002. Mrs. Olague was the wife of Cruz Olague.

Pekral, Melvin. Interview by author, December 1999. Rev. Pekral served as pastor of First Baptist from 1961–83.

Rammer, Jane. Interview by author, November 1994. Ms. Rammer was a skater on the Las Vegas strip in the late 1970s.

Ramy, Ted. Interview by author, November 2001. Rev. Ramy came to Dove Ministries in the late 1980s and followed John Perenti to Meadows Fellowship. Ted pastored Meadows when Perenti resigned.

Redburn, Duke. Interviewed by author, November 2001. Mr. Redburn was a Board member of Calvary Chapel Las Vegas from 1986–88.

Reid, Jim. Interview by author, January 1995. Rev. Reid was the self-designated Chaplain of the Strip. He held Bible Studies for entertainers.

Robeck, Cecil and Berdetta. Interview by author, April 1994. Cecil Robeck served as pastor of Trinity from 1954–56.

Rodriguez, David. Interview by author, October 2002. Mr. Rodriguez is the son of Albert and Jessie Rodriguez.

Rogers, James. Interview by author, February 1996. Rev. Rogers has pastored Greater New Jerusalem Baptist Church since 1984. He also served as head of the local chapter of the NAACP from 1996–2000.

Discussion Group. Interview by author, August 2000. This discussion group consisted of five women who have been longtime members of Cox's Upper Room Church of God in Christ. Their names are Georgette Franklin, Francis Harris, Ethel Cox, Louise Miller, and Alberta Davis.

Round Robin. Interview by author, August 2000. This meeting consisted of former members of Calvary Chapel/Dove Ministries. It included Joe and Bonnie Roush, Duke and Judy Redburn, and Taffy Lakatos.

Rowberry, David. Interview by author, February 2000. Dr. Rowberry is the director of the Las Vegas Institute of Religion on the campus of UNLV.

Sharp. Bill. Interview by author, January 2002. Rev. Sharp was pastor of Trinity Temple from 1972–74.

Ship, Donna. Interview by author, December 2001. Mrs. Ship has been an active member of Pilgrim Church of Christ Holiness since the 1940s. Her father, Rev. George Harris, held a pastoral role at the church from 1940–71.

Souza, Vita. Interview by author, September 1992. Mrs. Souza was active at Trinity since the early 1950s. She was Women's Ministries director during the 1960s.

Steward, Melvin and Norma. Interview by author, October 1994 and January 2002. Rev. Steward pastored Trinity from 1974–84.

Tyler, Evelyn. Interview by author, May 1992. Rev. Tyler pastored East Las Vegas Assembly of God from 1977 until her death in 1993.

Wagenknect, Hilda. Interview by author, April 1992. Rev. Wagenknecht was Trinity's record keeper from 1975–98.

Ware, Verna. Interview by author, July 2000. Mother Ware was the church mother of Pentecostal Temple Church of God in Christ from 1970–90. She was appointed state church mother in 1994.

Walsh, Pat. Interview by author, November 2000 and January 2001. Rev. Walsh was the founding pastor of Calvary Chapel Las Vegas and continued as its head into the early 1990s.

Wood, Kay. Interview by author, April 1992. Mrs. Wood was a professional singer until coming to Trinity in the 1960s.

Articles and Documents

Anon. *Annual Homecoming*. Las Vegas: Pentecostal Temple Church of God in Christ, 1985.

————. "City, Hank Greenspun Arrive at Land Sale Agreement," *Henderson Home News*, November 16, 1971.

————. "Dove Ministries Sued Over Wrongful Death." *Las Vegas Sun*, January 4, 1989

————. "Evangelist Kuhlman Draws LV Multitude." *Las Vegas Sun*, May 4, 1975.

————. "Fall Kills Worker at Dove Ministries." *Las Vegas Sun*, January 29, 1987.

————. "File for City Council," *Henderson Home News*, March 30, 1970.

————. "Mayor Questioning Outside Activities of City Employees." *Henderson Home News*, October 4, 1973.

————. "An Open Letter to the Sheep at Meadows Fellowship . . ." *Las Vegas Review Journal*, November 18, 1989.

————. "Oppose Consolidation." *Las Vegas Sun*, November 5, 1973.

————. "Welcome Back." *Las Vegas Sun*, April 13, 1971.

Associated Press. "Nevada Trails States in Religious Adherence." *Las Vegas Review Journal*, October 2, 1982.

————. "Utah Most Religious State." *Las Vegas Review Journal*, July 27, 1974.

Beall, Christopher. "Dove Ministries Conducts Baptism on Las Vegas Strip." *Las Vegas Review Journal*, August 24, 1986.

Breger, Jack. "Authority Votes 'Freebie' For Evangelistic Crusade." *Las Vegas Review Journal*, September 28, 1977.

Billy Graham Evangelistic Association. Official statistical records of crusades from 1976–1982. Field Ministries: P.O. Box 9313, Minneapolis, MN.

Black, David. "The Strip Minister, " *Gallery*, June 1976.

Bradley, Richard. "Las Vegas and the Mormons." BBC video aired on television in the United States on 5 January, 2000.

Brown, Mandy. "Minister to Casino Strip." *Kansas City Star*, September 8, 1974.

————. "Minister to Las Vegas Sin Row, That's Jim Reid." *Sunday Oklahoman*, Summer 1974.

Calvary Chapel Organizational Sheet. Las Vegas: Calvary Chapel Las Vegas, 1986.

Chandler, Russell. "Preacher Ministers to Vegas Strip," *Los Angeles Times*, March 24, 1974.

Cooper, Ron. "Room Service? Send 3 Bourbon, 2 Scotch—And One Chaplain." *Wall Street Journal*, May 21, 1974.

Cox tapes, Mother's Day 1967 and February 1969. These tapes of Bishop Cox's sermons belong to Mrs. Ethel Cox, sister-in-law to the late Bishop C. C. Cox.

Diocean Directory. Las Vegas: Diocese of Las Vegas, 1998.

Earl, Marion. *The History of the Las Vegas First Ward*. Earl's typed history of the Mormons in Las Vegas, no publisher, n.d.. Mr. Marion came to Las Vegas in 1932. He was the first counselor of the First Ward and also served the LDS church as a counselor.

Echoes of Faith. *Homecoming Roundup, 18th Anniversary Celebration 1989*. Las Vegas: Echoes of Faith, 1989.

Fiftieth Anniversary. Las Vegas: Trinity Temple, 1989.

Fiftieth Jubilee 1941–1991. Las Vegas: Pentecostal Temple Church of God in Christ, 1991.

First Baptist Church. 50th Anniversary, 1924–1974. Las Vegas: First Baptist Church, 1974.

Fredrick, Sherman. "Billy Graham Crusade Off to a Local Start," *Las Vegas Review Journal*, September 17, 1977.

———. "Fast Living Pastor Oversees Bankrupt Church." *Las Vegas Review Journal*, September 30, 1979.

———. "Graham Choir Director Talks," *Las Vegas Review Journal*, February 3, 1978.

———. "Graham Crusade Packs Center for 3rd Night," *Las Vegas Review Journal*, February 4, 1978.

———. "Graham Crusade Unites Local Churches," *Las Vegas Review Journal*, January 29, 1978.

———. "Graham Expects Mormons at Crusade," *Las Vegas Review Journal*, January 31, 1978.

———. "Overflow Crowd Hears Graham," *Las Vegas Review Journal*, February 2, 1978.

George, Dustin. "Stories of the Old West, " *The Nevadan*, July 13, 1969.

Galatz, Karen. "Graham Arrives in Las Vegas 'To Proclaim Gospel.'" *Las Vegas Sun*, January 31, 1978.

Heider, Timothy. "Ex-pastor of Dove Ministries Faces Trial." *Las Vegas Sun*, May 18, 1989.

Higgenbotham, Bud. Personal diary, entries from 1979 through 1981. Rev. Higgenbotham was the founding pastor of Grapevine Fellowship.

Historical Department. A letter dated March 10, 2000, from the Church of Jesus Christ of Latter Day Saints and signed by senior archivist Ronald G. Watt.

Jones, Betty. *Christ Church Episcopal 1907–1982*. Las Vegas: Christ Episcopal Church, 1982.

Kastelic. James. "Records Set During Nevada Crusade." *Las Vegas Review Journal*, 12 June, 1980.

King, Archbishop J. *Discipline of Christ Holy Sanctified Church of America*. No publisher listed, n.d.

LaVella, Phil. "Pastor Pleads Guilty to Fraud Charges in Dove Ministries Scandal." *Las Vegas Review Journal*, December 21, 1989.

Marshall, Dwight. *First United Methodist Las Vegas In Celebration of 65 Years*. Las Vegas: First United Methodist Church, 1970.

Marshall, Karen. "Las Vegas Chaplain Winning the Loser." *Chicago Daily News*, November 8–9, 1975.

———. "Praising God on the Las Vegas Strip." *St. Louis Globe Democrat Sunday Magazine*, September 21, 1975, 6–7.

McCoy, B. Elizabeth. *McCoy Autobiography*. Las Vegas: Echoes of Faith Ministries, April 2001.

McVey, Sean. "A Matter of Love," *Las Vegas Sun*, February 3, 1978.

Memorandum. Las Vegas: Diocese of Las Vegas, November 20, 2001. The diocese office provided a copy of the annual report sent to Rome. The report consisted of statistical information from 1995–2000.

Minutes. Trinity Temple official board minutes from 1974.

Modzelewski, Teresa. "That Godspell Magic, " *The Nevadan*, November 11, 1973.

New Dimensions Magazine. Las Vegas: New Dimensions Ministries. Published by Rev. Bill Sharp during his years as pastor of Trinity Temple, n.d.

Newburn, Dan. "Graham Surprised By Las Vegas' Response." *Las Vegas Sun*, February 6, 1978.

Obsequies. Clyde Carson Cox memorial service, February 7, 1969.

Pappa, Erik. "Christian College Mulls Broad Series of Courses." *Las Vegas Sun*, February 9, 1987.

Pictoral Directory: Calvary Church of the Foursquare Gospel. Dallas: McKee, 1971.

Press Release. Copy of the history of Mormons from the Las Vegas Nevada Institute of Religion, International Research, P.O. Drawer A. Silver City, NV, 1992.

Reeves, Allen. "Huge Land Sale Looms for 'Little People.'" *Henderson Home News*, June 22, 1971.

Rice, Ann. "Minister to the Strip, " *The Nevadan*, October 6, 1974.

School. Clyde C. Cox Elementary, Dedication, Open House. Program brochure, February 5, 1988.

Second Baptist Church. *The History of Second Baptist Church*. Las Vegas: Second Baptist Church, 1991.

Squires, Delphine. *Christ Episcopal Church: The Way We Were*. Las Vegas: Christ Episcopal Church, 1997.

Steward, Melvin. "A Good Mother: A Bible Definition." Mother's Day message preached by Rev. Steward at Trinity on May 11, 1975.

———. "Modern Mothers." Mother's Day message preached by Rev. Steward at Trinity on May 13, 1984.

St. Louis Globe Democrat Sunday Magazine, September 21, 1975.

Sunday School records. Bishop Herman Ishmael of Christ Holy Sanctified Church allowed the viewing of Sunday School records which dated the beginning of the church's history as 1952.

Tell. "Trinity's Envoy of Light and Life." Las Vegas: Trinity Temple, n.d.

"This Is Great Country." *The Nevadan*, April 15, 1968.

Trinity Temple Annual Report, 1984. This was the year the Nybakkens came to pastor Trinity. There is no record of CPC support before they came.

Vincent, Bill. "St. James, the Little Church with Many Seeds." *The Nevadan*, May 11, 1975.

Walsh, Pat. *Marriage, Divorce & Remarriage*. Las Vegas: Hallelujah Fellowship, n.d.

Warner, Wayne. "Remembering Evangelist Kathryn Kuhlman." *Pentecostal Evangel*, February 2003, 29.

Weier, Anita. "Business Group Puts God on Agenda." *Las Vegas Review Journal*, June 23, 1986.

———. "Pastors at Las Vegas Church Step Down." *Las Vegas Review Journal*, November 24, 1987.

———. "Scandal, Financial Woes Hurt Ministry." *Las Vegas Review Journal*, August 2, 1987.

Zion United Methodist Church. 78th Anniversary Celebration. Las Vegas: Zion Methodist Church, November 10, 1995.

Government Documents

Congressional Record, Proceedings and Debates of the 105th Congress, First Session, March 13, 1997, vol. 143, No. 32.

Proclamation. By Mayor Robert Groesbeck of Henderson, NV, March 12, 1997.

Proclamation. By Governor Bob Miller of the state of Nevada, March 3, 1997.

Proclamation. By the Latin Chamber of Commerce, Las Vegas, NV, March 15, 1997.

U.S. Department of Commerce, Bureau of the Census, Census of Population, 1910–1980.

Newspapers

Atlanta Journal and Constitution, February 11, 1978.
Chicago Daily News, November 8–9, 1975.
Henderson Homes News, see notes for specific dates.
Kansas City Star, September 8, 1974.
Las Vegas Age, see notes for specific dates.
Las Vegas Review Journal, see notes for specific dates.
Las Vegas Sun, see notes for specific dates. Los Angeles Times, March 24, 1974.
New York Times, October 7, 1973.
Richmond-times Dispatch, October 8, 1973. Sunday Oklahoman, Summer 1974.
Wall Street Journal, May 21, 1974.

SECONDARY SOURCES

Anderson, Robert Mapes. *Vision of the Disinherited the Making of American Pentecostalism* New York: Oxford University Press, 1979.
Balmer, Randall. *Mine Eyes Have Seen the Glory.* New York: Oxford University Press, 1989.
Barna, George. *What Americans Believe.* Ventura, CA: Regal, 1991.
Barrett, David. *World Christian Encyclopedia.* New York: Oxford University Press, 2001.
Biumhofer, Edith L. *The Assemblies of God: A Chapter in the Story of American Pentecostalism*, Vol. 1—to 1941. Springfield, MO: Gospel, 1989.
Bonhoeffer, Dietrich. *Life Together.* New York: Harper & Row Publishers, 1954.
Burgess, Stanley, Gary McGee, and Patrick Alexander. *Dictionary of Pentecostal and Charismatic Movements.* Grand Rapids: Zondervan, 1988.
Conkin, Paul. *American Originals.* Chapel Hill, NC: University of North Carolina Press, 1997.
Cox, Harvey. *Fire from Heaven.* Reading, MA: Addison-Wesley, 1995.
Dayton, Donald. *Theological Roots of Pentecostalism.* Grand Rapids: Asbury, 1987.
Fee, Gordon D. *God's Empowering Presence.* Peabody, MA: Hendrickson, 1994.
Friedmann, Robert. *The Theology of Anabaptism.* Scottsdale, PA: Herald, 1973.
Genovese, Eugene. *Roll Jordon Roll.* New York: Pantheon, 1974.
Hagan, William. *American Indians.* Chicago: University of Chicago Press, 1979.
Harrell, David Edwin. *Oral Roberts: An American Life.* San Francisco: Harper & Row, 1985.
Hatch, Nathan. *The Democratization of American Christianity.* New Haven, CT: Yale University Press, 1989.
House, Adrian. *Francis of Assisi.* Mahway, NJ: Hidden Spring, 2000.
Johnson, Paul. *A Shopkeeper's Millennium.* New York: Hill & Wang, 1978.
Knox, Ronald A. *Enthusiasm.* Westminster, MD: Christian Classics, 1983.
Lindsey, Hal. *The Late Great Planet Earth.* Grand Rapids: Zondervan, 1970.
Lowman, Zelvin. *A Voice in the Desert.* Franklin, TN: Provident, 1992.
Marsden, George. *Fundamentalism.* New York: Oxford University Press, 1980.
Matthews, Donald G. *Religion in the Old South.* Chicago: University of Chicago Press, 1977.
McLoughlin, William. *Billy Graham: Revivalist in a Secular Age.* New York: Ronald, 1960.
Menzies, William. *Anointed to Serve.* Springfield, MO: Gospel, 1971.
Moehring, Eugene. *Resort City in the Sunbelt.* Las Vegas: University of Nevada Press, 1995.

Moore, Laurence. *Selling God: American Religion in the Marketplace of Culture*. New York: Oxford University Press, 1994.

Moynahan, Brian. *The Faith*. New York: Doubleday, 2002.

Niebuhr, H. Richard. *Christ and Culture*. New York: Harper & Row, 1951.

———. *The Social Sources of Denominationalism*. New York: New American Library, 1975.

Paher, Stanley. *Las Vegas, As It Began, As It Grew*. Las Vegas: Nevada, 1971.

Pearlman, Myer. *Knowing the Doctrines of the Bible*. Springfield, MO: Gospel, 1981.

Poloma, Margaret M. *The Assemblies of God at the Crossroads*. Knoxville, TN: University of Tennessee Press, 1989.

Reid, Jim. *Praising God on the Las Vegas Strip*. Grand Rapids: Zondervan, 1975.

Shepard, Charles. "Forgiven, " New York: Atlantic Monthly, 1989.

Scott, R. B. Y. *The Relevance of the Prophets*. New York: Macmillan, 1968.

Synan, Vincent. *The Holiness-Pentecostal Tradition*. Grand Rapids: Eerdmans, 1997.

Vaughn, John. *The World's Twenty Largest Churches*, Grand Rapids: Baker, 1984.

Wacker, Grant. *Heaven Below*. Washington, DC: Howard University Press, 2001.

Weber, Timothy. *Living in the Shadow of the Second Coming*. Chicago: University of Chicago Press, 1987.

Wuthnow, Robert. *The Struggle For America's Soul*. Grand Rapids: Eerdmans, 1989.

———. *The Restructuring of American Religion*, Princeton: Princeton University Press, 1988.

About the Author

Dr. Steward was lead pastor of Calvary Community Church in Las Vegas from 1990–2004. He is Professor of History Emeritus at Bethany University in Santa Cruz, California. From 2005–2011 Dr. Steward was chairman of the Social Sciences Department at Bethany. Dr. Steward received his bachelor's degree at Point Loma University, his Master of Divinity and Master of Theology degrees from Princeton Theological Seminary, and a Doctor of Philosophy degree in American history from the University of Nevada, Las Vegas.